W9-CPF-435

PRAISE FOR *ESTATE PLANNING TO DIE FOR*®

"Sally demystifies a complex topic. She provides a road map for navigating the challenging, but rewarding, estate planning market."

Morey Stettner
Contributor, Investor's Business Daily

"In American Skandia's second year in the variable life insurance business, we were rated #1 in the industry in education and marketing material, in large part due to our working with Sally."

Patti Abram
Past Marketing Director, American Skandia

"Legalese becomes plain English in this book."

Donald Murray
Columnist, The Boston Globe

"This book captures all the excitement of Sally's dynamic presentations. It's no surprise she's one of our most sought-after speakers. We consider her to be the industry's expert on estate planning."

Lyn Fisher
President, Financial Forum Speakers Bureau

"I wish Sally had written this book years ago! It should be required reading for new and seasoned advisors alike."

Paul Buckley, Jr.
Speaking Captain, Million Dollar Round Table

Estate Planning To Die For®

....

AN INSIDER'S GUIDE FOR FINANCIAL PROFESSIONALS

SALLY MULHERN, J.D.

Estate Planning To Die For®

An Insiders Guide For Financial Professionals

Second Edition

ISBN: 0-9779129-1-4

LCCN: 2006902484

Cover Design: Vital Design, Portsmouth, New Hampshire

Cover Photo: Images Photography Studio, Port Orange, Florida

Printed by Odyssey Press Inc., Gonic, New Hampshire

DEDICATION

To Patrick and James, who make it all worthwhile.

CONTENTS

DISCLAIMER AND DISCLOSURE

The material in this book is intended to provide you with guidance regarding estate planning. It does not constitute, and should not be treated as, legal advice regarding the use of any particular estate planning technique or the consequences associated with any such technique. Although every effort has been made to assure the accuracy of this material, the author does not assume responsibility for any individual's or entity's reliance on the written information contained in the book. You should independently verify all statements made in the book before applying them to a specific situation, and should independently determine both the tax and non-tax consequences of using any particular estate planning technique before recommending that technique to a client or implementing it on a client's or your own behalf.

Some of the names and facts listed in this book have been changed to protect identities and to preserve client confidentiality.

Circular 230 Disclosure: U.S. federal tax advice in the book was not intended or written to be used, and cannot be used, by any person for the purpose of avoiding tax penalties that may be imposed with respect to the matters addressed. Some of that advice may have been written to support the promotion or marketing of the transaction(s) or matter(s) addressed within the meaning of IRS Cir-

cular 230, in which case, be advised that the advice was written to support the promotion or marketing of the transaction(s) or matter(s) addressed, and you should seek advice based on your particular circumstances from an independent tax advisor.

ACKNOWLEDGEMENTS

To begin, I would like to thank all the financial professionals who purchased the first edition of this book. Your commitment to learning how to become an effective member of the estate planning "team" continues to inspire me.

My husband and law partner, David, also deserves special recognition. Not only did he and our paralegal, Hayley Stone, spend hours updating the book to reflect recent changes in the law, but he continues to be the best lawyer, spouse, and father I know.

After reading the first edition, Patti Abram gently reminded me that summer camps are where children go for recreation when they are not in school, and that summer homes are what families fight over. Her sage counsel is always appreciated, and I'm honored to continue to call her my friend. Another friend, Andrea Hansen, has always believed in me, for which I am very thankful.

Tad, Martin, Karen, and Judy at Odyssey Press, Inc. have provided endless guidance and support, for which I am eternally grateful.

Both of my sons have now completed college (one also has a Master's Degree), for which I am also eternally grateful, and very proud. Their willingness to let me share stories about them in this book, and in my presentations, has been commendable. They are the other loves of my life.

Last, but not least, my sincere thanks to all of the clients of Mulhern & Scott. David and I continue to be honored with their loyalty and trust.

Introduction

—

THE SIX RULES FOR SUCCESS

I have one simple goal in writing this book: To give you the confidence and tools necessary to serve estate planning clients effectively as a financial professional. In the process, I want to teach you how to become a valued member of the estate planning "team" and inspire you to provide client-centered services. I assure you, if you achieve this, you will be well rewarded financially and—more importantly—in the satisfaction of knowing that you have provided services that have made a real difference to your clients and their families.

Many of the concepts in this book may be unfamiliar to you at first. Tax law, in particular, is arcane and often challenging. As you will see, however, learning the fundamentals is a very achievable goal, and you don't need to know everything!

Many of you (those who are honest!) may say, "Estate planning has never interested me." Even more of you may say, "Estate planning is way too complicated. There's too big a learning curve for me to be interested in working in this area."

What I **want** you to say after reading this book, however, is, "Estate planning is an exciting challenge. Now I know I can really do something useful and profitable in this field."

My 25+ years as a practicing estate planning lawyer have taught me that you can achieve this by following six simple rules:

1. Assemble the right estate planning "team"

2. Establish yourself as the "go to" advisor

3. Tackle the fundamentals

4. Focus on client goals—sales will follow

5. Embrace Uncle Sam

6. Communicate! Communicate! Communicate!

If you apply these rules properly, you will be well on your way to becoming a successful financial professional in the estate planning field. In the process, you'll develop strong client relationships based on having provided truly valuable service.

Let's get started!

Chapter One

—

RULE #1

ASSEMBLE THE RIGHT ESTATE PLANNING "TEAM"

Effective estate planning requires that all allied professionals (lawyers, insurance agents, accountants, financial advisors, trust officers, and charitable development advisors) work together as a "team." When the strengths of all team members are combined, the whole is always greater than the sum of the parts. Conversely, if the allied professionals make contradictory recommendations as part of the estate planning process, the client will be confused and will hesitate to move forward.

About two years ago, a close friend of mine, "Donna," was very sick. She went to her primary physician, who told her, "You must do X." Then she went to a specialist, who said, "You can't do X; that would only make things worse. You must do Y." And guess what she did? Nothing!

That is exactly what happens in the estate planning process. If the accountant recommends one thing, and the lawyer recommends another, the client will throw up his or her hands and say, "Hey, if the experts can't agree, then how should I know what to do?" The client is poorly served, and the opportunity for effective planning is squandered.

ADVANTAGES TO THE "TEAM APPROACH"

In addition to providing consistent recommendations, there are three other advantages to the team approach in estate planning, particularly for financial professionals.

■ ADVANTAGE #1: YOU DON'T NEED TO KNOW IT ALL!

First, the team approach to estate planning means you don't personally need to know everything about estate planning. But you do have to link up with estate planning attorneys who do. This is great news—you should already feel relieved! You don't need to be intimidated by the generation-skipping transfer tax, retirement benefit disclaimers, or grantor-retained annuity trusts. You don't have to take on that huge learning curve!

■ ADVANTAGE #2: OTHER TEAM MEMBERS CAN MAKE UNBIASED PRODUCT RECOMMENDATIONS

Second, other members of the team can provide objective suggestions for using financial products as an integral part of the client's estate plan. For example, if the attorney recommends the purchase of a life insurance policy as part of the estate plan, the client will appreciate having received an unbiased opinion, and will be more likely to move forward. This happens routinely in my practice. Recently, while being interviewed for a financial services magazine, I endorsed the team approach to estate planning. Astutely, the interviewer, Nicole, asked me, "Doesn't it bother you that other members of the team, most notably the financial advisors, are in a position to earn more than you do?" At first, the question took me aback. Perhaps sensing my hesitation, Nicole said, "But I guess it's all about the client, isn't it? It's about doing a good job for the client." She was exactly right! We can never forget that, ultimately, it is all about the client.

Therefore, it goes without saying that my recommendations regarding a product purchase are, without exception, based exclusively on the clients' needs. It is essential for financial advisors to appreciate that there will be times when it is the attorney's professional and ethical obligation to abide by and secure the client's wishes not to move forward with purchasing an insurance or other financial product. If you fail to respect an attorney's professional obligation in this regard, it will only work to your disadvantage. Let me share an example from my personal practice.

One day, a life insurance agent asked me to meet with two of her clients to assess their estate planning needs. After meeting with the clients, I recommended repeatedly that each of them purchase a sizeable life insurance policy. Both clients needed the policies in order to provide liquidity to pay estate taxes. Both clients, however, told me point-blank that they did not want to purchase the insurance. Although I disagreed with their decisions, I felt I had fully explained the consequences for their estate planning, and it was ultimately their call.

When I informed the agent, she was dumbfounded. I can understand why, because both clients clearly needed the insurance. Unfortunately, the agent didn't leave it there. She got very angry—not at the clients' decision, but at me personally. She told me I had to push them to change their minds. I refused, and I immediately decided never to work with her again. The very next life insurance referral I made involved the sale of the largest life insurance policy a client of mine has ever purchased. Needless to say, I sent the case to another insurance agent.

The moral of this story is simple: Respect the attorney's professional obligations, and be patient. If a client decides not to purchase a product, or not to follow your recommendation in spite of an attorney's advice, don't kill the messenger. If you do, the messenger will knock on someone else's door next time.

The idea of respecting the attorney's professional obligations has another dimension: the attorney-client privilege. Often, this prohibits the attorney from even explaining to the other team members why the client opted not to buy a particular product or follow certain recommendations. Let me share another example from my practice.

A few years ago, an investment advisor, "Mr. X," referred a husband and wife to me for estate planning. The couple was new to the area, and had already met with Mr. X about managing their investment portfolio. At our first meeting, the couple told me they had decided not to retain Mr. X. They said they were going to work with someone at another brokerage firm, but they didn't want me to tell Mr. X because they didn't want to hurt his feelings. They said they just weren't going to return his calls. After I told them I didn't feel comfortable with that approach, they agreed to call him and tell him.

A few months later, I got a call from Mr. X. He was irate. He said he'd heard that the clients had gone to another investment manager, and asked me to confirm whether it was true. Unfortunately, I couldn't confirm or deny it. To do so would have violated the attorney-client privilege. What the couple told me could not be shared with anyone without their consent. When I told Mr. X that I couldn't respond, he got even more upset, saying that he had referred the clients to me in the first place. I told him I would have the clients call him, which I did. Needless to say, it was an uncomfortable situation. Although the advisor ultimately recognized that I was bound by the professional code of ethics, it didn't remove the sting. I've never received another referral from him.

■ ADVANTAGE #3: YOU MAY RECEIVE CROSS-REFERRALS

The third advantage to the team approach for financial professionals is the possibility of cross-referrals. Again, however, I offer a word of caution. You need to be realistic about the number of clients that an estate planning attorney will be able to refer to you. When I'm approached by advisors interested in joining my team, I make three things very clear:

✓ They will have much more opportunity to refer clients to me than I will have to refer clients to them. Most of my clients are financially successful and need my services as a direct result of their current relationships with competent, responsible financial advisors. They typically already have an insurance agent, an investment advisor, and an accountant. By comparison, few people have an existing relationship with an attorney concentrating in estate planning.

✓ Those clients I do refer, however, typically will have substantial needs. What I lack in cross-referral quantity, I usually make up for in quality.

✓ Assuming I provide good legal services to a financial advisor's clients, the clients will be happy, which will ultimately be a good reflection on the advisor. Conversely, clients unhappy with an attorney often blame, and fire, the referring advisor.

WHERE TO FIND A GOOD ESTATE PLANNING LAWYER

Often, clients and other members of the estate planning team don't know how to find a qualified estate planning attorney. In fact, the question I receive most often from people attending my estate planning presentations is, "Can you give me the name of a good estate planning attorney in my area?" I tell them all the same thing: Go to **www.actec.org**, the website for The American College of Trust and Estate Counsel (ACTEC). To be an ACTEC member, an attorney must, among other things, have been in trust and estate practice for at least ten years and have received the highest ethical rating. The website enables users to search for member attorneys by geographic area, which is particularly helpful.

Another good way to find competent estate planning lawyers is to join your state or local estate planning council. The councils typically meet monthly or quarterly, and are a great way to meet allied professionals in the estate planning field. In addition, you might want to call your state bar association and ask for a listing of upcoming estate planning seminars. These seminars are continuing legal education courses, and the attorneys presenting are typically highly respected. Attending the seminars is also a great way to learn more about the issues involved with estate planning, from the basic to the advanced.

Not every estate planning attorney is a good fit with every client. Therefore, I encourage you to establish a team relationship with two or three estate planning attorneys. When I first started practice, I looked very young (coincidentally, that was also before I had children!). I thought clients would shy away from working with me on account of my age and presumed inexperience. Exactly the opposite was true, however. I found that many clients preferred to work with me because they figured I would still be in practice when they died.

Of course, now that I'm a more seasoned (i.e., old!) practitioner, what I make up in experience I lose in longevity. Now, clients discreetly ask me what would happen if something happened to me; in other words, they want to know about my business succession plans. One week my husband and I had three young lawyers independently call us to say they wanted to talk with us about joining our firm, with an eye toward taking over the practice. This also happened to be the second week after my younger son left for college, which didn't sit well with me. I remember looking at my husband and saying, "We must really be looking old. Maybe our gray hairs aren't as beneficial to our practice as we thought!"

The point is, develop team relationships with a number of competent estate planning lawyers. When selecting an estate planning lawyer, clients look for different qualities, depending on their various goals and assumptions, rational and irrational. You will provide a service to your clients by offering them a choice of competent estate planning attorneys.

WHAT MAKES A GOOD TEAM MEMBER?

Advisors repeatedly ask me how I choose my team members. They want to know what qualities I look for in accountants, financial planners, investment advisors, bank trust officers, and insurance agents. The question always bothered me, because I never really had a good answer. It's never been something I could quantify; it's always been something I've felt, more than I've known.

All that changed one morning in Dallas. I was giving a presentation with the national spokesman for a global financial institution. Jim told the audience that, in his experience, clients choose to work with a particular advisor based on three things:

> 1. They *like* the advisor;
>
> 2. They *trust* the advisor; and
>
> 3. The feel the advisor *adds value*.

Suddenly, I had my answer! The same is true of how I pick my team members.

First, I have to like the advisor as a person. I'm reluctant to admit this, but it's absolutely the very first factor I look to when screening potential team members. I only have so many hours in my work day, and I have a choice: I can spend those hours with people I enjoy, or with ones I don't. It's that simple.

Suppose I'm introduced to two equally competent trust officers. The first has absolutely no sense of humor and takes no discernible interest in me, my family, or the world. The second is engaging, makes me laugh, and enjoys talking about things other than work. Which one of the two do you think I would want on my team? Which one do you think I would prefer to put in front of a valued client?

I'll let you in on a little secret. I have an unwritten rule when I go to lunch with other financial professionals. I call it the "dessert rule," meaning that I prefer not to discuss business until the dessert arrives after the meal. The rest of the time, I like to get to know the person. Admittedly, in some situations, I have to bend the rule a little, in which case it becomes the "main course rule." If the lunch has been set up as a working lunch, and more time is needed to discuss substantive matters, the business discussion can begin over the lasagna, tuna sandwich, or chicken pot pie. Under no circumstances, however, should it ever become anything short of the "salad rule." You need at least until the salad arrives to chat. In my opinion, bringing up business before that time shows you're interested only in the deal, not in the people involved in the process.

I remember one investment manager who invited David and me to lunch. We had never met him before. "George" had just left a big brokerage house to start his own firm, and David and I agreed to meet him for lunch a few weeks later. I don't think I'd even sat down at the table before George whipped out his firm brochure. It was all glossy and quite impressive. But it was already too late, because he'd already lost both of us.

For the next 90 minutes, all David and I wanted was to get away. Throughout lunch, George talked about P/E ratios (which, to this day, I still think has something to do with high school gym class), he showed us colorful graphs (which I couldn't, and never want to, understand), and he told us how successful he'd been at the big company. He never noticed my eyes glazing over. He never sensed that David and I wanted to bolt. He was in his own little world. He couldn't even make it to the "menu rule." When we got back to the office, David looked at me and laughed. He said, "Never make me go out with that guy again!" I never have.

There is one good thing you can take from the "George" example, however. I, in common with many seasoned estate planning lawyers, am always interested in meeting someone who's starting out on their own. I respect their courage, but it also brings back memories. My husband and I started our own firm, in a new city, without a single client, about 20 years ago. I often say I don't know if we were naïve, or just plain stupid. We had two children under the age of three, a tiny apartment, and nothing could hold us back. Those were some of the happiest days of my life.

Our business plan was simple: We got a post office box. We figured that while we walked the six blocks to and from the post office, we'd run into people we knew who might need legal services. Believe it or not, it worked. So did sponsoring public seminars with accountants, insurance agents, bankers, and brokers. If asked, I would tell you that I believe there's an entrepreneurial gene, detectable only by those who carry it. I have the gene, so does my husband, and, although flawed in his approach, so did "George." If you're new in the business, or are considering going out on your own, keep this in mind. There are many professionals who will welcome the opportunity to help you.

In contrast to George, here is an example of a good interpersonal experience with a team member. I enjoy working with John, another investment advisor. I met John about 15 years ago. We have many mutual clients, some of whom he's generously referred to me, and some of whom I've referred to him. He, David and I have a wonderful professional relationship, but, over the years, we've also developed a personal one. He's taken the time to make that happen. As a result, I know about John's wife and children. I know he ran with the bulls in Pamplona for his 50th birthday. I've been on his boat, and I know he likes to fish. Once, I had a client who needed an investment advisor. At the first meeting I learned the client liked to fish, so I sent him to John. They hit it off famously. I look forward to the times John and I work together, and that's why he's part of my estate planning team.

In writing this book, a fourth, and very important, quality came to mind in defining what I look for in a good team member. He or she must be genuinely concerned about the client. Lena is an excellent example.

A year or so ago, I referred clients to Lena for help with their investments. It was immediately clear that she was providing competent financial advice, but, after a few months, something else came to my attention. Mr. "X" was older, and it took him extra time to process financial information. Lena's patience and meticulous attention to detail in explaining issues to Mr. X was extraordinary. Her tireless commitment to making sure that Mr. X grasped the necessary financial concepts in a dignified manner proved to me that Lena truly cared about Mr. X. As a result of that experience, I now feel even better that Lena is part of my team.

Chapter Two

—

RULE #2

ESTABLISH YOURSELF AS THE "GO TO" ADVISOR

I'm sure you all remember the rhyme,

"Rich man, poor man, beggar man, thief;

doctor, lawyer, Indian chief."

I think of this rhyme when I see financial professionals, particularly those who are new to the industry and trying to develop a client following. Their first instinct is to contact doctors and lawyers, because they assume doctors and lawyers are wealthy, and, therefore, in need of their services. Unfortunately, doctors and lawyers are often the worst prospects. In my experience, doctors are so busy that they often have difficulty finding time to commit to the estate planning process. As for lawyers, suffice it to say that many of them are like the cobblers whose children have no shoes.

I believe that there is a better potential client identified in the rhyme. Most of you will be surprised by who it is: It's the Indian chief! By "Indian chief," I mean someone who is a decision-maker, a leader, possibly in charge of a large number of people, and facing ongoing economic and organizational decisions, including providing for his or her successor.

When seeking new clients, it's important that you look beyond income figures and net worth statements. In my opinion, it's best to focus on (i) specific client needs, and (ii) particular estate planning issues. The goal is to establish yourself as the "go to" person when a client has that particular need or faces that particular issue. Let's look at examples of each.

FOCUSING ON SPECIFIC CLIENT NEEDS

First, let's look at business development based on specific client needs. I find that two groups have particular needs that often make them ideal estate and financial planning clients:

(a) People who own their own businesses, and

(b) People with substantial real estate holdings.

Not only do these individuals need wills, trusts, financial powers of attorney, and advanced health care directives, but they also need counsel regarding business succession and tax planning. For example, suppose a business owner passes away with $1,000,000 due to the IRS in estate tax. The heirs may have to sell the business, possibly at a distress sale, in order to pay the tax within the requisite nine months. Even if an arrangement can be made with the IRS for payment over time, it may prove to be a financial strain that threatens business continuity and the family's financial security.

Fortunately, a number of estate planning vehicles are available to avoid that result. It's possible to minimize the tax or generate the requisite liquidity to pay the tax. In addition, it's likely that the business owner will need to establish a retirement plan, implement a funded buy-sell agreement, purchase life insurance to provide liquidity to fund the inheritance for children not involved in the business, buy long-term care insurance, and consider discounted gifting of the business to the next generation. In such a scenario, financial professionals who are part of the estate planning team are likely to do well.

A few years ago a financial advisor, Dennis, set up an appointment to stop by my office. He wanted to introduce himself and show me some seminar materials his company had put together. The thing that really impressed me about Dennis's materials was that they dealt with a very specific topic: business succession. Dennis wasn't trying to appeal to the masses. He'd decided to target a particular audience and educate them about the cost of not moving ahead with their estate planning. Although I don't do many local presentations, I was so impressed with Dennis's approach that I agreed to speak at his next seminar. It was a huge success. We've done a number of seminars together since then, and I credit the success of each of them to one thing: Dennis's ability to focus on a particular client need.

FOCUSING ON PARTICULAR ISSUES

Second, let's look at business development based on particular estate planning issues. Below is a list of some of the issues particularly relevant to estate planning (most of which are discussed in greater detail under Rule #3: "Tackle the Fundamentals"). You might want to focus on one or more of them:

- **Net Unrealized Appreciation (NUA)** – Clients with employer stock in their 401(k) plans are entitled to special income tax treatment.

If the employer stock is withdrawn from the 401(k) and transferred into a brokerage account (rather than rolled into an IRA), ordinary income tax is due only on the original cost basis. When the employer stock is subsequently sold, any appreciation is subject to capital gains tax, not ordinary income tax.

For example, suppose employer stock in a 401(k) has a cost basis of $5,000, and a fair market value of $100,000. If the employer takes a lump sum distribution from the 401(k) and transfers the employer stock into a brokerage account, this is what happens:

✓ Ordinary income tax is immediately due on $5,000; and

✓ When the client subsequently sells the employer stock, the remaining $95,000 is subject to capital gains tax, not ordinary income tax.

Unfortunately, most clients are never told the employer stock in their 401(k)s qualifies for special NUA treatment. They are typically told to roll the lump sum distributions from their 401(k)s into IRAs. In my experience, it is probably the #1 issue missed by advisors when working with clients.

A few years ago, a new client came in to see me. "Susan" had just taken early retirement from GE. She had a $2,000,000+ IRA, which had been rolled over from her 401(k). I asked her if she had a financial advisor. She said she did. I asked her if she had met with her advisor prior to rolling the 401(k) into the IRA. She said she had. I was really bothered by her situation. Ultimately, Susan will pay significantly more tax on her retirement assets because the NUA issue wasn't identified.

Please be sure to put NUA on your radar screen! It's a fabulous "go to" advisor issue, and it presents a wonderful opportunity for you to distinguish yourself as a valued member of the estate planning team.

- **Non-citizen spouses** – Special planning is required for lifetime gifts and use of the unlimited marital deduction at death.

- **"Blended" marriages** – Numerous estate planning issues are involved, particularly if there are children by prior marriage(s).

- **Charitable planning** – Many clients can actually pass more on to their beneficiaries at death by donating assets to charity either during their lifetime or at their death.

- **Land conservation** – Individuals with valuable real estate may be interested in preserving the land from future development and in bringing down the value of the land for estate tax purposes.

- **Closely held businesses** – Business owners face unique business succession, retirement, creditor protection, and tax issues, as well as concerns regarding "equalization" of inheritance for children not involved in the business.

- **Beneficiaries with special needs** – Assets must be left to beneficiaries with special needs in carefully drafted trusts, so that the beneficiaries do not lose their governmental assistance benefits.

- **Long-term care** – I expect this market to explode as baby boomers get older and states make qualifying for Medicaid more restrictive.

- **Summer homes** – Some of the worst intra-family fights I've seen in my practice have involved the distribution of family summer homes. Comprehensive lifetime planning and creation of post-death liquidity can help ease the transition.

I want to give you an example of someone who knows about the last issue, summer homes.

After one of our business succession seminars, Dennis and I had lunch. Because of the "dessert rule," I learned that Dennis and his wife own a summer home. Dennis told me he was struggling with the best way to leave the home to his four children, because he didn't want the children to fight about it after he died.

We discussed a number of alternatives and agreed that he should consider leaving the summer home to his children in trust, with provisions governing use and payment of expenses. We also talked about the purchase of a second-to-die life insurance policy. The proceeds of the policy could be added to the trust and used to pay the summer home's expenses, thereby eliminating (we hoped) fights over payment of expenses. It was a great lunch. I got to know Dennis as a person, and I was also able to see how his mind works when tackling an estate planning problem.

Ever since that lunch, when possible, if I have an estate planning client who owns a summer home, I bring in Dennis as part of the team. He's my "go-to" guy on that issue. I know he's not only competent on the financial issues regarding summer homes, but also empathetic about the emotional ones. It's been a great fit for clients.

If someone can be a specialist in passing on summer homes, imagine the other possibilities!

Once you have experience with a specific estate planning issue, let your local attorneys, accountants, brokers, insurance agents, and other estate planning professionals know. Publish an article in the local newspaper or in a trade magazine, or give a presentation highlighting your expertise. If you don't have an area of expertise, go develop one. Select an issue that interests you, and go learn everything you can about it. Affiliate with other team members interested in the issue. Send them professional articles about the topic, and share experiences from your practice with them. Arrange for you and the other team members to meet for a "brown bag lunch," or meet once or twice a year on the golf course or at a spa, to discuss recent developments associated with the issue. Make the issue challenging and fun!

A year or so ago, a convenience store in my town sold a multi-million dollar winning lottery ticket. Even after a week, the winner had not come forward. Many people speculated that the winner was meeting with an attorney. In that regard, I was interviewed by the local newspaper about the estate planning issues associated with lottery winnings. A few weeks later, my husband and I were approached by a Cape Cod newspaper to comment on another lottery winner story. Since that time, we routinely get inquiries from people across the country about estate planning for lottery winners. At one point, if you "Googled" me, you would see references to my work with lottery winners. Even my parish priest mentioned it! It's a perfect example of how a particular client need, footnoted in a small local story, can explode into a world of opportunity.

Chapter Three

—

RULE #3

TACKLE THE FUNDAMENTALS

The key word here is "fundamentals." In order to be a valued member of the estate planning team, you don't have to know everything about estate planning, but you do have to have a working knowledge of the basics.

THE THREE GOALS OF ESTATE PLANNING

I believe most clients have three goals in estate planning. The first two are pretty straightforward:

1. Avoid the cost and delay of probate; and

2. Minimize taxes.

The third goal is more nuanced. It was brought to my attention by a client. After acknowledging that he wanted to pass on as much as possible to his children in an efficient manner, the client said it was also important to him that his children not look forward to his dying. I call this goal,

3. Avoid the "Menendez Problem."

Here's what you need to know about all three goals:

■ GOAL # 1: AVOID THE COST AND DELAY OF PROBATE

"If you look forward to going to the dentist or paying taxes,
you'll love probate."[1]

In recent years there has been a widespread trend in estate planning to structure the transfer of assets at death in a manner that avoids the probate process. In light of the expense of probate, this preventive measure can yield substantial savings.

Probate is the process whereby, when someone dies, certain of his or her assets are submitted to the jurisdiction of the Probate Court in the county in which that person lived at the time of his or her death. Typically, the custodian of the Will must deliver it to the Probate Court shortly after the decedent's death.

Then, often many things must occur before the assets can be distributed, including:

✓ The Probate Court judge must approve the written formalities of the Will;

✓ a Petition for Appointment of Fiduciary must be filed with and granted by the Probate Court;

✓ assets must be appraised and inventoried;

✓ a bond must be posted;

✓ all individuals and entities with a beneficial interest in the estate must be notified, and annual accounts must be rendered...*then* the final distribution takes place.

---

1   "The Multipurpose Trust," *Modern Maturity*, August-September 1991

Probate is required whether a person dies with a Will (i.e., *testate*) or without a Will (i.e., *intestate*). The fiduciary of a testate estate is often referred to as the "*executor*" or "*personal representative*," and the fiduciary of an intestate estate is often referred to as the "*administrator.*" When a person dies testate, the terms of the Will, reflecting as they do the express intent of the decedent, control the distribution of assets.

When a person dies intestate, the law establishes a framework based on degree of kinship. This framework determines who will be the beneficiaries of the estate, without reference to any intent of the decedent. Each state has its own specific rule of intestate distribution.

With limited exceptions, the probate procedure is typically quite costly and lengthy. Obviously, the availability of the estate's assets can be a critical issue to the beneficiaries during this period.

➤ The Three Ways to Avoid Probate

There are three principal ways to avoid probate:

- ● *Joint Tenancy with Rights of Survivorship*

  Property owned by two or more individuals as joint tenants with rights of survivorship (JTROS) passes by law to the surviving joint tenant(s) immediately upon another joint tenant's death. No probate is required.

  The advantages of JTROS are that it's simple and inexpensive. Suppose Winkin, Blinkin and Nod own a house together as joint tenants with rights of survivorship. When Winkin dies, Blinkin and Nod automatically become the owners as surviving joint tenants. When Blinkin dies, Nod automatically becomes sole owner as surviving joint tenant. Put simply, with JTROS, the last person standing takes all.

Here are the disadvantages of JTROS:

1) Upon the death of the last surviving joint tenant, probate is required. In my prior example, when Nod dies, the house would have to go through probate. Also, JTROS assets do not avoid probate upon simultaneous death. Under those circumstances, the law typically presumes that each JTROS owner owns a pro-rata fraction of the asset involved. So, from my prior example, if Winkin, Blinkin and Nod all died simultaneously, each of them would be deemed to own 1/3 of the house, and each 1/3 share would have to go through probate.

2) JTROS assets cannot be used to fund the credit shelter Trust (i.e., A/B Trust planning), so federal estate tax planning is thwarted (See "**Goal #2: Minimizing Taxes**," below).

3) JTROS assets only get a partial step-up in basis upon the first death. For example, suppose Husband and Wife buy stock worth $100,000 in 2007, and take title as JTROS. When Husband dies in 2009, the stock passes automatically to Wife as surviving joint tenant. The stock is worth $200,000.00. Wife's tax basis in the stock is now $150,000. Only half of the value of the stock gets a step-up in basis as of Husband's date of death. If Wife sells the stock for

$200,000, she will pay capital gains tax on $50,000. (*Note*: EGTRRA ["The Economic Growth and Tax Relief Reconciliation Act of 2001"], enacted June 7, 2001, limits the amount of step-up in basis at death in 2010 to $1,300,000 per decedent, plus an additional $3,000,000 for assets passing to surviving spouse).

- ### Assets with Beneficiary Designations

Clients can designate beneficiaries on their life insurance policies, retirement accounts, and annuities. As a result, these assets don't have to go through probate.

Designating the correct beneficiary for liquidity and income tax purposes is discussed below. NEVER let a client name his or her "estate" as beneficiary on a life insurance policy, retirement account, or annuity. If the "estate" is designated as beneficiary, assets that would otherwise automatically avoid probate will have to go through probate. In addition, there can be significant adverse tax consequences (see **Tax #4: Income Tax**, below) Be sure your clients designate an individual, organization, or trust as beneficiary. This, of course, should be done in conjunction with the estate planning attorney's recommendations.

- ### Revocable Trusts

Increasingly, clients are using Revocable Trusts to avoid probate. A Revocable Trust is a "Will substitute." It becomes the primary document of a client's estate plan, and controls who inherits the client's assets (other than those with a beneficiary designation) upon the client's death.

Most importantly, assets held in a Revocable Trust at the time of a client's death avoid the cost, delay, and public exposure of probate. This is particularly valuable when a client owns real estate in more than one state. In the absence of a Revocable Trust, probate would be required in each state where real estate is located.

The key word here is "revocable." A Revocable Trust can be amended or revoked at any time by the client who set it up, assuming he or she is competent. Generally, the client is the trustee of his or her Revocable Trust, and, therefore, no separate income tax return is required. Everything is reported on the client's 1040. The client retains complete control over the Revocable Trust, including the right to change the trust beneficiaries.

Because the client retains complete control over his or her Revocable Trust, assets in the trust are subject to the client's creditors. If a person is sued, assets in his or her Revocable Trust are at risk. This comes as a surprise to many clients. They think that because they've put their assets in the Revocable Trust, the assets are creditor-protected. Not true. Only assets in an *irrevocable* trust are creditor-protected. That is because clients give up all control and "incidents of ownership" over assets in an irrevocable trust. (Figure 1)

Often, you will hear a Revocable Trust referred to as a *Revocable Living Trust*. This is because Revocable Trusts are set up during a client's lifetime. Compare this to *testamentary trusts*, which come into effect only when the client dies. Young couples typically set up testamentary trusts in their estate planning documents so that, if they

TYPES OF TRUSTS

REVOCABLE
- "Living Trust"
- Can be amended
- Set up during lifetime
- Used to avoid probate
- Subject to creditors' claims

IRREVOCABLE
- Can't be amended
- Set up during lifetime or comes into effect at death
- Used to avoid estate tax and for creditor protection

TESTAMENTARY
- An irrevocable trust that comes into effect at death
- Includes "Ferrari" trusts

Figure 1

die prematurely, their young children's inheritances will be held in trust until they turn a certain age. I recommend a minimum age of 30, and refer to this type of testamentary trust as a "Ferrari" trust. Let me explain.

I have two young sons. I was talking to one son, James, recently about my own estate planning, and mentioned that if David and I died, James's share of our assets would be held in trust for him until he turned 30. Prior to age 30, he could request money from the trustee (my sister) for his education, health, money for a down payment on a house, money to start a business, etc. I told him I'd done that so he wouldn't be able to run out and buy a Ferrari. He admitted that he probably *would* go out and buy a Ferrari if he had the chance. As a result, I increased his age of distribution to 35!

◆ Be Sure Clients Fund Their Revocable Trusts!!

I have a major pet peeve: Revocable Trusts that are never funded. This means that a client has set up a Revocable Trust, but has never completed the necessary paperwork to make sure that the assets that would otherwise have to go through probate are retitled in the name of the Revocable Trust. Typically, it's not the client's fault. Either they were never told they needed to fund the Revocable Trust, or they were never told how to do the funding.

Recently a new client came to see me. Another attorney had set up a Revocable Trust for her 15 years ago. However, her home, rental property, securities, and personal property were still in her own name. I told her that the attorney who set up the Revocable Trust had "sold her a car without an engine." If she had died, because the assets were still in her name, they all would have had to go through probate. The primary purpose for which she had established the Revocable Trust would have been defeated.

After a client signs his or her estate planning documents, I send him or her home with a "Revocable Trust Funding Summary." It instructs the client what he or she needs to do to retitle assets in the name of his or her Revocable Trust, and to change beneficiaries on life insurance, retirement accounts and annuities. With the client's permission, I also send a copy of the summary to each team member. That way, I know everyone has the same information.

One way in which you can make yourself a valued team member is to establish yourself as an integral part of the funding process. To do so, you must first educate yourself about what's involved and what the estate planning attorney is trying to accomplish. Then, you should offer to handle as much of the funding paperwork for the client as possible.

I recall an experience with "Bill," an accountant. I'd mailed him a mutual client's Revocable Trust Funding Summary, and he called to take issue with certain of my recommendations. To begin, he told me I'd failed to tell the client that she needed to apply for a federal tax identification number now that she had a Revocable Trust. Bill was wrong about this because the client was the trustee of her Revocable Trust, and could report all trust income on her 1040, using her Social Security number. In addition, Bill said that the Revocable Trust (i) *should* not be listed as beneficiary of the client's life insurance, and (ii) *could* not be listed as beneficiary on the client's IRA. I wasn't too upset because I knew that Bill had not been involved with many estate planning clients.

The first thing I did was fax him a simple funding diagram. (Figure 2)

I like this diagram because it shows the basic funding process. It's really just a decision tree. The first question is:

"Does this asset allow a beneficiary designation?"

If the answer is "no" (such as with real estate, securities, business interests, and personal property), then the asset has to be titled in the name of the Revocable Trust to avoid probate.

If the answer is "yes" (such as with life insurance, retirement accounts, and annuities), then we go on to the second question:

"Is this asset subject to income tax after the client dies?"

If the answer is "no" (such as with life insurance), then the asset should list the Revocable Trust as beneficiary, unless there are extenuating circumstances. By listing the Revocable Trust as beneficiary of life insurance policies, the proceeds can be used to pay debts and

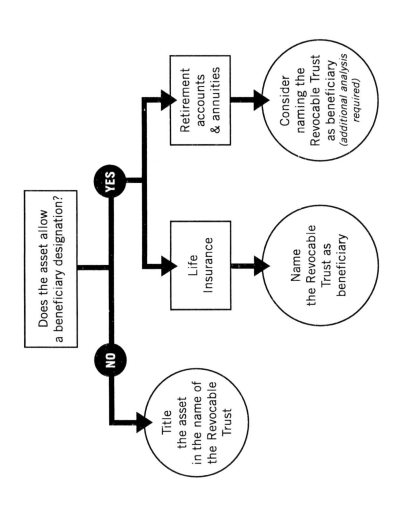

Figure 2

expenses, and can be applied to the decedent's credit shelter trust, in order to take advantage of federal estate tax planning.

If the answer is "yes" (such as with retirement accounts and annuities), then it's *possible* the Revocable Trust should be named as beneficiary, but additional analysis is required (e.g., "stretch" IRA planning considerations—see below).

I walked Bill through the funding process, and everything was fine—until he called me a few months later about another mutual client. On the Revocable Trust Funding Summary, I'd instructed the client to list her Revocable Trust as beneficiary of her life insurance. Bill was calling to let me know that he'd told the client to list her husband as beneficiary of the insurance. This created two big problems.

First, Bill confused the client. That's a fatal mistake if you're a member of my team. If an advisor has a problem with a team member's recommendation, it's crucial to discuss it with the team member directly.

NEVER, EVER, SHOULD THE CLIENT
BE PUT IN THE MIDDLE,
UNSURE OF WHAT TO DO.

Second, by naming her husband as beneficiary of the insurance policy, the client wasted the opportunity for federal estate tax planning. Had the life insurance beneficiary not been changed in the end from the husband to the Revocable Trust, the client could potentially have paid an additional $1,000,000 in estate tax.

Compare Bill with Susan. Susan started as an advisor about five years ago. She's very intelligent and devoted to her clients. The thing that really struck me about Susan when we began working with mutual clients was her extraordinary commitment to learning about the funding process and making sure she and I came up with solutions that met my needs as well as those of her company's compliance department. The first time I mailed Susan a Revocable Trust Funding Summary for a mutual client, she scheduled a 15-minute conference call so the two of us could go over exactly what I wanted to accomplish, and why. She asked how she could make the funding process easier for me. I told her one of the best things she could do was help the clients fill out and submit the funding paperwork, including the Change of Beneficiary Forms for the clients' IRAs. She agreed to do so.

About a week later, Susan called to let me know her company had some questions about the IRA Change of Beneficiary Forms. I had included sophisticated disclaimer language in the beneficiary designations, and Susan had been told the company's standard Change of Beneficiary Forms couldn't accommodate the "non-traditional" language.

After I explained to her the importance of the disclaimer beneficiary designation for estate and income tax purposes, Susan went back to her compliance department. She was able to determine that they were not concerned about the language fitting on the form, but rather about potential liability if, due to the complexity of the beneficiary designation, they distributed the IRA to the wrong beneficiary. Susan and I came up with a simple solution. At the end of the beneficiary designation, I added language holding the company harmless in distributing the account to the beneficiaries identified by the client's representative after death. Problem solved.

Ever since that first client, I've welcomed the opportunity to work with Susan. I know she understands what's involved in the funding process and is committed to working efficiently with clients in completing the requisite paperwork.

◆ Clients With Revocable Trusts Still Need Wills!!

Even though I said a Revocable Trust is a "Will substitute," clients with Revocable Trusts still need Wills. This type of Will is often called a *"pour-over Will"* because it provides that any asset (other than beneficiary-designated assets) not already in the Revocable Trust at the time of death "pours over" into the Revocable Trust. In short, the Revocable Trust is the beneficiary under the Will.

I think of a Will, used in conjunction with a Revocable Trust, as a "safety net." The Will "catches" anything not in the Revocable Trust when the client dies, and pours that asset over into the Revocable Trust for distribution in accordance with the terms of the Revocable Trust. If a client retitles all assets that would otherwise have to go through probate in the name of his or her Revocable Trust prior to death, probate can be avoided altogether.

Sometimes, due to extenuating circumstances, probate is required because an asset falls outside the Revocable Trust. For example, we had a client on the first plane on 9/11. He had set up a Revocable Trust, and all of his assets (including real estate, a business, stocks, and personal property) had been retitled in the name of his Revocable Trust. If he had died of natural causes, we would simply have notified the probate court that no probate was necessary. However, in this case, there was an asset that we couldn't have put in the Revocable Trust before the client died: his share of the government's victim compensation fund. His right to collect under the fund literally sprang into effect the moment he was killed. When his estate received his share of the fund, the amount collected went through probate, "poured over" to his Revocable Trust, and was distributed to his family in accordance with the terms specified in his Revocable Trust. The "safety net" Will did its job.

◆ Other Estate Planning Documents

This "pour-over" Will feature, together with the Revocable Trust, is displayed in the "Diagram of Estate Planning Documents" on the next page (Figure 3). The diagram also lists the other documents that are a necessary part of every client's comprehensive estate plan.

DIAGRAM OF ESTATE PLANNING DOCUMENTS

(PROBATE)

POUR-OVER WILL
- Should name executor and successor executor
- Should name guardian and successor guardian
- Pours over remaining assets into existing Revocable Trust after probate
- Accommodates cause of action arising at death

REVOCABLE TRUST
- Controlled by Grantor
- Remains private
- Avoids probate (cost & delay)
- Covers simultaneous death
- Permits professional management of assets if desired (e.g., investments)
- Permits orderly distribution of funds
- Allows step-up in basis
- Is distributed immediately on death
- Provides for incapacity
- Allows for A-B Trust planning

DURABLE POWER OF ATTORNEY
- Is effective immediately (consider safeguards)
- Works with trustee of Revocable Trust
- Should provide for gifting and for funding of Revocable Trust

LIVING WILL / TERMINAL CARE DOCUMENT
- (Provide client with wallet insert)

DURABLE POWER OF ATTORNEY FOR HEALTH CARE / HEALTH CARE PROXY
- (Provide client with wallet insert)

Figure 3

Of course, all estate planning documents prepared for a client must comply with state law. It's crucial that you work with an estate planning attorney competent in that regard.

> *Durable Power of Attorney*

This document authorizes an individual or individuals to act on the client's behalf with respect to financial matters, even if the client subsequently becomes incompetent. This includes writing checks and signing tax returns. The document is effective immediately upon signing, unless a *Springing Durable Power of Attorney* (i.e., one that becomes effective only upon the client's becoming incompetent) is used. The primary purpose of this document is to avoid guardianship proceedings in the event the client becomes incompetent.

Because a Durable Power of Attorney is effective while the client is still alive, and because it grants so much control to the individual(s) designated to serve on the client's behalf, it's very important that you, and other members of the estate planning team, establish appropriate safeguards to prevent any potential abuse. For example, we have our clients sign a letter instructing our office not to release the original or an authenticated copy of the Durable Power of Attorney unless one of our attorneys contacts the client, while he or she is still competent, to be sure the client knows the document is being used.

This practice proved invaluable about seven years ago. The daughter of a client came in, requesting a certified copy of her mother's Durable Power of Attorney. Daughter told me Mom didn't want to do her banking anymore because of her age, and had asked Daughter to take things over for her. Daughter said she needed a certified copy of Mom's Durable Power of Attorney to take to the bank. I told Daughter that, because of the letter Mom had signed, I would need to call Mom to get her authorization to release the Durable Power of Attorney. When I called Mom, she knew nothing about Daughter coming in to get the certified copy. Needless to say, we nipped a real problem in the bud. The next day, Mom came in to sign a new Durable Power of Attorney appointing another child to act on her behalf.

One important thing for you to know about Durable Powers of Attorney is this: If a Durable Power of Attorney does not include express authority to make gifts, any gift made pursuant to the Durable Power of Attorney within three years prior to the client's death will be brought back into the client's taxable estate for federal estate tax purposes. Unfortunately, many Durable Powers of Attorney just contain a general statement granting an individual authority "to do everything I could do myself." Admittedly, this is better than nothing, but it falls far short of a competent job.

Years ago, I got a call from a team member, "Joe." He told me a mutual client, "Mary," was dying of cancer. I had not even known Mary was ill. Joe called me because he wanted to check whether there was anything that needed to be done with Mary's estate planning before she died. In fact, there was. At that time, the federal estate tax exclusion was $650,000, and Mary's net worth was about $700,000. She had four children and three grandchildren. One daughter, "Carol," was designated to act on Mary's behalf in Mary's Durable Power of Attorney. Within 48 hours of Joe's call, I had arranged for Carol to make $10,000 gifts (the annual exclusion amount at the time) to herself and each of Mary's other children and grandchildren, for a total of $70,000. As a result, when Mary died, because her net worth was only $630,000 (i.e., $700,000 - $70,000), both estate tax and the filing of an estate tax return were avoided.

I knew the amount gifted by Carol would not be "pulled back" into Mary's estate because I had drafted Mary's Durable Power of Attorney to include the requisite gifting clause. Had the clause *not* been included, when Mary died, the $70,000 would have been included in her federal taxable estate, and her estate would have owed approximately $20,000 in federal estate tax. I made sure the family understood it was Joe's initiative in calling me that saved them the money.

I'd like to make one last point about my experience with Joe. It did not surprise me that he knew about Mary's illness, while I did not. Joe met with Mary routinely to discuss her investments and prepare her income tax returns. I, on the other hand, spoke with Mary only when she called me with a specific question or wanted me to make changes to her estate planning documents. Understandably, she saw me as an expense item. Given that you, like Joe, will often be the team member with the most access to a client's financial and personal information, you will often be in the best position to alert the other team members, including the attorney, if the client's situation changes. This positions you as an essential player in the ongoing estate planning process.

> ### *Living Will (Terminal Care Document)*

This is often referred to as the "pull the plug" document. The client is authorized to direct his or her physician to withhold or withdraw life support, including a feeding tube, if he or she is incompetent and either: (i) suffering from a terminal illness (from which he or she will die but for artificial intervention), or (ii) in a permanent vegetative state.

> ### Durable Power of Attorney for Health Care (Health Care Proxy)

This document designates an individual or individuals to make *routine* health care decisions in the event the client is incompetent to do so.

> ### Notice of Existence of Living Will and Durable Power of Attorney For Health Care

Our office gives each client a laminated wallet insert with the following language:

IMPORTANT NOTICE

I have a signed a Terminal Care Document (Living Will) and Durable Power of Attorney For Health Care on file with my attorneys, Mulhern & Scott, PLLC of Portsmouth, New Hampshire (xxx) xxx-xxxx. Please contact Mulhern & Scott, PLLC immediately if I am unable to express my own wishes regarding medical decisions, including, but not limited to, the utilization of life-sustaining procedures and/or the administration of artificial hydration and nutrition.

We recommend clients clip the wallet insert to their driver's license, so if they're ever in an accident and taken to an emergency room, the medical staff will know that the Living Will and Durable Power of Attorney For Health Care exist.

Even wallet inserts can be a source of amusement. A few years ago "Fred," age 90+, was in the process of clipping the insert to his license when I noticed his license didn't authorize organ donation. When I asked Fred if he wanted to be an organ donor, he looked at me like I was crazy and said, "Who in the world would possibly want my organs?" As delicately as possible, I told Fred his body would probably go right up Route 89 to Dartmouth Medical School, to be used by a first-year medical student. Without missing a beat, his son, sitting at the far end of the table, said, "Go for it Dad. You always wanted to go to the Ivy League!"

■ GOAL #2: MINIMIZE TAXES

There are five taxes that need to be considered for estate planning purposes:

1. Federal Estate Tax

2. State Death Tax

3. Capital Gains Tax

4. Income Tax

5. Generation-Skipping Tax

It's important that you understand the application and implication of each.

➤ Tax #1: Federal Estate Tax

The federal estate tax is imposed at the time of death. Under EGTRRA, the tax rate is scheduled to remain stable at approximately 45% over the next few years.

● *Federal Estate Tax Exclusion*

Every individual has the ability to shelter a specified amount from federal estate tax at the time of his or her death. This amount is referred to as the federal estate tax exclusion. At the time this second edition goes to press (in 2009), it is unclear what the likely future amount of these exclusions will be. As you will see from the next chart, the law provides for a generous exemption in 2009, an estate tax repeal in 2010, and a much lower exemption in 2011. It seems likely that the new administration and Congress will re-visit this issue, and that the estate tax will remain in effect. What is presently unknown, however, is just what the revised federal estate tax exclusion amount and federal estate tax rate will be. Under current law, the exclusions are:

Year	Exclusion
2009	3,500,000
2010	No Federal Estate Tax
2011	1,000,000

Practitioners were shocked when these exclusion amounts were imposed by EGTRRA in 2001. In contrast, I decided to have some fun with it, realizing that there are two medical implications to the ever-changing exclusion.

First, people are going to want to be kept alive artificially until they can die in a year when they won't have to pay estate tax. Suppose, for example, it's 2009. Mrs. Terminally Ill has a $4,500,000 estate and is on life support. If the plug is pulled, her estate will owe $450,000 in federal estate tax. By contrast, if the plug isn't pulled until 2010 (when there is no federal estate tax), there won't be any estate tax liability. In light of this, I joke that my clients will want "contingent" Living Wills, instructing their physicians not to pull the plug until they can die in a year when no federal estate tax would be due!

The second medical implication is the reverse of the first. In 2010, when there is no estate tax, there's going to be a massive power surge as every plug is pulled across the nation.

Something else was scheduled to happen in 2010; that was the year Jack Kevorkian was supposed to get out of jail! He was paroled early, but will still be available to pull life-support plugs.

Enough fun. Let's get back to the federal estate tax.

- ### *Unlimited Marital Deduction ("A/B Trust" Planning)*

In addition to the federal estate tax exclusion, any amount can go to a surviving spouse federal estate tax free. This is referred to as the "unlimited marital deduction."

In order for a married couple to take advantage of both of their federal estate tax exclusions, however, they must set up certain estate tax provisions in their estate planning documents before either of them dies. This planning is often referred to as "A/B Trust" planning or "Credit Shelter/QTIP (Qualified Terminable Interest Property) Trust" planning.

Let's look at an example:

Suppose Harry and Beatrice Smith have an $8,000,000 estate. If Harry dies in 2009 leaving everything to Beatrice, no estate tax will be due at the time of his death, regardless of the value of the assets in Harry's name. Any amount in Harry's name in excess of the federal estate tax exclusion will pass estate tax free to Beatrice because of the unlimited marital deduction.

However, when Beatrice dies, there will be a problem. She will have $8,000,000 in her name, and, assuming her federal estate tax exclusion is only $3,500,000 (i.e., she dies later in 2009), the portion of her estate that will be subject to federal estate tax will be $4,500,000 (i.e., $8,000,000–$3,500,000). Approximately $2,025,000 of estate tax will be due. A significant portion of the tax is triggered because, by leaving everything outright to Beatrice, Harry never used his federal estate tax exclusion. He wasted it. (Figure 4)

NO FEDERAL ESTATE TAX PLANNING

ASSETS = $8,000,000

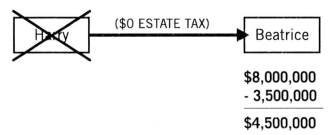

$8,000,000
- 3,500,000
_____
$4,500,000

ESTATE TAX = $2,025,000

Figure 4

How, then, should the Smiths have done their estate planning to take advantage of both exclusions? They should have used "A/B Trust" planning, so that when Harry died, the assets in his Revocable Trust were divided into two subtrusts. The first subtrust, commonly referred to as the "B" Trust or "Credit Shelter Trust," would be funded with assets equal to Harry's available federal estate tax exclusion. The second subtrust, commonly referred to as the "A" Trust, "Marital Trust," or "QTIP Trust," would be funded with all assets remaining in Harry's Revocable Trust, after funding the "B" Trust.

Beatrice and the children would be the beneficiaries of the "B" Trust. (Occasionally clients list either the spouse or one or more of the children as beneficiaries. This is true, for example, where the "B" Trust holds subchapter S stock. In that case, the "B" Trust, among other limitations, can have only one income beneficiary in order to qualify as a "qualified subchapter S Trust," or "QSST".) They could receive trust income and principal, based on specified standards, typically tied to their health, education, and living needs. By law, Beatrice must be the sole beneficiary of the "A" Trust (because of the unlimited martial deduction), and would have to receive all trust income annually. She could also receive distributions of trust principal based on her health, education, and living needs.

The reason to create an A/B Trust plan in this case is that, when Beatrice dies, none of the assets remaining in the "B" Trust will be includable in Beatrice's federal taxable estate. Only what remains in the "A" Trust, together with what Beatrice has in her own name, will be subject to estate tax. Assuming Harry has $4,000,000 in his name, and $3,500,000 goes into the "B" Trust upon Harry's death, when Beatrice dies, only $4,500,000 would be includable in her taxable estate (i.e., the $500,000 in the "A" Trust, plus the $4,000,000 in Beatrice's name). After we subtract Beatrice's $3,500,000 exclusion (assuming she dies later in 2009), only $1,000,000 would be taxable, and the estate tax due would be approximately $450,000. By using both exclusions, the estate tax has been reduced from $2,025,000 to $450,000. This is a $1,575,000 savings. (Figure 5)

A/B TRUST PLANNING
TAKING MAXIMUM ADVANTAGE
OF ALLOWED EXCLUSIONS

ASSETS = $8,000,000

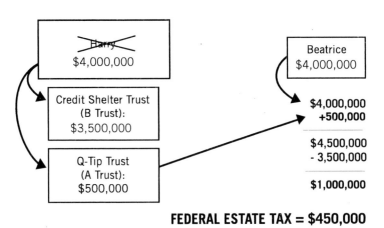

Figure 5

I mentioned earlier the importance of funding clients' Revocable Trusts. With A/B Trust planning for married individuals, the amount funded in each Revocable Trust is crucial. Both the husband and wife should have sufficient assets in their individual Revocable Trusts so that, regardless of the order of death, they each can use their federal estate tax exclusion. In other words, be sure that, in a taxable estate, each member of the couple uses his and her exclusion amount to the extent possible.

Let's go back to our example. Suppose the Smiths set up their estate planning documents with A/B Trust planning, and, after funding, Harry has $7,000,000 in his Revocable Trust and Beatrice has $1,000,000 in hers. If Beatrice dies first, even with A/B Trust planning, her credit shelter trust can only be funded with $1,000,000. If the federal exclusion is $3,500,000 (as is the case in 2009), she will have wasted $2,500,000 of her available federal estate tax exclusion. This imbalance in the funding of their respective trusts will cause the imposition of approximately $1,575,000 in taxes on the estate, which is $1,125,000 more than if they had "equalized" the amounts in the two trusts. (Figure 6)

When funding their Revocable Trusts, the Smiths should have equalized their assets between the two Revocable Trusts. They should have transferred assets between the two of them (which is possible because of the unlimited marital gift tax exclusion for U.S. citizen spouses) so that they each ended up with at least $3,500,000 in their own Revocable Trust.

A/B TRUST PLANNING
WITH PARTIALLY WASTED EXCLUSION

ASSETS = $8,000,000

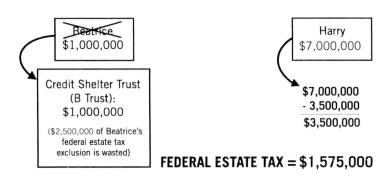

Figure 6

Of course, this is not always possible, given, for example, limitations on ownership of life insurance and retirement accounts. At minimum, however, with limited exceptions regarding retirement accounts (see below regarding disclaimer planning), it's important that neither Harry nor Beatrice have assets in excess of the federal estate tax exclusion amount until the other of the two of them has assets at least equal to the exclusion amount.

In summary, with A/B Trust planning for married couples, no federal estate tax is due until the second death, and then only to the extent the combined values of the then remaining "A" Trust and the second spouse's assets exceed the then available federal estate tax exclusion.

There's a second advantage to A/B Trust planning. It solves the potential "Sven The Tennis Pro" problem. If Harry dies first, leaving his assets outright to Beatrice, he has no guarantee that Beatrice will ultimately leave everything to their children. If Beatrice inherits Harry's money outright, all of a sudden Sven, the tennis pro, may start offering Beatrice free tennis lessons. He might get real friendly with her, realizing that Beatrice could leave everything to him and his children. This wouldn't be possible with A/B Trust planning, however, because, upon Beatrice's death, whatever remains in the "A" Trust and "B" Trust goes to the beneficiaries originally specified in Harry's Revocable Trust. Presumably, these would be Harry's children. With A/B Trust planning, Harry, in effect, controls "from the grave" where the "A Trust" and "B Trust" assets go upon Beatrice's death.

Women, don't worry. A/B Trust planning also solves the "Casserole Lady" problem. I know this from first-hand experience. My mom predeceased my dad. The day of my mom's funeral, a woman showed up on my dad's doorstep, with a casserole in hand. I was relieved to know my mom's Revocable Trust included A/B Trust planning!

The joke is that when the law establishing A/B Trust planning passed in the early 1980s, so many members of Congress were divorced, they wanted a way to provide for their second spouses, but still be assured their assets would ultimately get back to their children from prior marriage. On behalf of my clients in second marriages, I'm here to tell you, A/B Trust planning works wonders.

- ### *Disclaimer Planning as an Alternative to A/B Trust Planning*

As the amount of the federal estate tax exclusion has increased over the past few years, more clients have opted for an alternative to traditional A/B Trust planning. That alternative is often referred to as "disclaimer planning.,"

The beauty of disclaimer planning is that it allows a married couple to fund a "B" or "Credit Shelter Trust" only if needed to avoid federal estate tax. It is particularly useful for clients with holdings in excess of $2,000,000 (the amount a married couple can pass on, estate tax free, under current law, as of 2011) but not in excess of $7,000,000 (the amount a married couple can pass on in 2009).

With disclaimer planning, a married couple sets up their estate planning so that, upon the first death, all the deceased spouse's assets go outright to the surviving spouse. The surviving spouse is given the option, however, to disclaim (i.e., say "no thank you" to, and refuse to accept) all or some portion of the assets that the deceased spouse has left to him or her. Any assets disclaimed by the surviving spouse go, instead, into a Credit Shelter Trust (i.e., the "B" part of traditional A/B Trust Planning), as provided in the deceased spouse's estate plan. The result is that disclaimer planning allows married couples to "wait-and-see" what their financial situation and the estate tax exclusion amount is at the time the first spouse dies. If, based on the then applicable estate tax exclusion, it appears that the couple's total assets are unlikely to be subject to federal estate tax at the second death, the surviving spouse can simply accept the deceased spouse's assets, and not fund the "B" Trust. By contrast, if it appears that such acceptance would likely lead to an estate tax at the second death, the surviving spouse can disclaim all or some portion of the deceased spouse's assets, in which case the disclaimed assets will pass into a "B" Trust.

Let's look at an example.

Suppose, for example, Joe and Karen Sixtysomething have an estate worth $3,000,000. Under current law, the use of one federal estate tax exclusion (for 2009, the federal estate tax exclusion is $3,500,000) would be sufficient to allow all of the Sixtysomethings' assets to pass to their heirs estate tax free. If Joe dies in 2009, and if his estate plan leaves all his assets outright to Karen (i.e., free of A/B Trust Planning), there would be no estate tax due if Karen dies in 2009 or 2010 (when the exemption is $3,500,00 and unlimited, respectively). However, if Karen dies in 2011 (when the exemption is scheduled to be only $1,000,000), a $900,000 estate tax liability would be triggered (i.e., $3,000,000 [Sixtysomethings' total estate] - $1,000,000 [exclusion used by Karen only] = $2,000,000 × 45% tax rate = $900,000).

This example highlights the fact that, on one hand, the Sixtysomethings don't want to set up A/B Trust Planning if it won't be needed. On the other hand, they don't want to trigger unnecessary estate tax liability.

As a solution, the Sixtysomethings could use disclaimer planning. They could set up their estate planning so that: (i) all assets go outright to the surviving spouse upon the first death, (ii) but any assets disclaimed by the surviving spouse will go into a "B" Trust created by the deceased spouse's estate planning documents. That way, the estate tax reduction provided by a "B" Trust is there if they need it, but the surviving spouse can accept all of the deceased spouse's assets, outright, if the surviving spouse determines that one estate tax exemption is reasonably likely to protect all of the couple's assets upon the surviving spouse's death. (Figure 6a)

DISCLAIMER PLANNING

ASSETS = $ 3,000,000

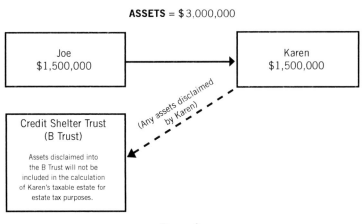

Figure 6a

Three caveats are in order with respect to disclaimer planning. First, in order to be a "qualified disclaimer" (i.e., one the IRS will accept).

First, the surviving spouse must make the disclaimer in writing, within nine months (unless otherwise specified by state law), must not have exercised control over the disclaimed asset, and must meet additional legal requirements. Clients need to have this time deadline, as well as the control restrictions and other legal formalities, carefully explained. Other disclaimer requirements may also apply under state law, and must be reviewed with clients.

Second, certain clients may not be candidates for disclaimer planning because it requires the surviving spouse to make a decision that he or she may not be able to make, particularly after having just lost a spouse (this might include elderly clients, the financially unsophisticated, or anyone else who would be ill-suited to make a timely qualified disclaimer).

Third, if the surviving spouse accepts the assets from the deceased spouse (i.e., does not make a disclaimer), all of the deceased spouse's assets are at risk in the event the surviving spouse remarries (something to be considered, for example, if the couple is young, or if there is a substantial age disparity between the spouses such that the survivor might be likely to remarry—remember Sven and the casserole ladies discussed above?!)

For these reasons, though very attractive for its flexibility, disclaimer planning does not fit all situations.

• *A/B Trust Planning with a Non-Citizen Spouse*

There's one final point that needs to be made regarding A/B Trust planning. Any amount left to a non-citizen spouse in excess of the death tax exclusion must be held in a "Qualified Domestic Trust," or "QDOT", as opposed to a QTIP Trust. The primary difference is that any principal withdrawn from a QDOT during the surviving non-citizen spouse's lifetime is immediately subject to federal estate tax. The rationale behind the QDOT is simple: The IRS does not want non-citizen spouses to withdraw the principal from a marital trust and move it to a country where it would not be subject to federal estate tax when the non-citizen spouse dies. It solves the "take the money and run" problem. (Figure 7)

To the extent it is anticipated that a non-citizen spouse will need to access principal in excess of the estate tax exclusion, liquidity, often in the form of insurance proceeds held within an ILIT, will be essential.

For QDOT purposes, a surviving spouse's status as a U.S. citizen or non-U.S. citizen is not determined as of the deceased spouse's date of death, but rather as of the date the decedent's federal estate tax return is filed.

NON-CITIZEN SPOUSE

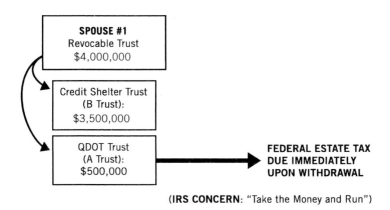

Figure 7

Therefore, if a non-citizen spouse wants QTIP (rather than QDOT) treatment to apply, he or she may want to consider applying for U.S. citizenship upon his or her spouse's death, and putting the decedent's federal estate tax return on extension until citizenship is granted.

● *What if Federal Estate Tax is Still Due?*

We've discussed the estate tax exclusion and unlimited marital deduction, but one very important question still remains: What if, as in the Smith example, there's still federal estate tax due? Is there anything else a single individual or married couple can do to minimize or plan for payment of the estate tax?

Most clients assume they have to "throw in the towel" and pay the tax, but that isn't the case. There are a host of planning opportunities available, including the following:

+ Gifting

+ Outright charitable giving and charitable bequests

+ Life insurance

+ Charitable remainder trust with wealth replacement trust

+ Testamentary charitable lead trust

+ Family limited partnership

+ Limited liability company

+ Qualified personal residence trust

✦ Grantor retained annuity trust

✦ Intentionally defective irrevocable trust

✦ Conservation easements

◆ **Gifting**

Each individual can currently give $13,000 per year to any number of individuals. This is known as the gift tax "annual exclusion amount." No gift tax return is required.

If a client gives more than $13,000 to an individual in a given year, however, a gift tax return needs to be filed. No gift tax is due, but the client "uses up" a portion of the federal estate tax exclusion that would otherwise be available upon his or her death. In the past, a client could use up all of his or her estate tax exclusion during his or her lifetime, but the law changed under EGTRRA. Now, each client has a lifetime gifting cap of $1,000,000, in addition to the annual gift tax exclusion.

Therefore, if a single client were to give $1,539,000 to his three children, this is what would happen:

• $39,000 would qualify for the annual gift tax exclusion (i.e., three children × $13,000 each)

• $1,000,000 would be exempt under the client's lifetime gifting cap

- $500,000 would be subject to gift tax, payable now, even though the federal estate tax exclusion is $3,500,000 in 2009.

With limited exception regarding non-citizen spouses, a married couple can gift $26,000, but if more than $13,000 comes from assets in either husband or wife's name alone, it's referred to as a "split gift," and a gift tax return must be filed for documentation purposes only. No gift tax is due, and neither husband nor wife uses any of his or her federal estate tax exclusion.

◆ Outright Charitable Giving and Charitable Bequests

Any asset given outright to charity during one's lifetime, or left to charity at death, is exempt from federal estate tax.

◆ Life Insurance

Life insurance proceeds are often used to pay estate tax, particularly when a client owns illiquid assets, such as real estate or a business, which would otherwise have to be sold at a distress sale to pay the tax.

› *Six Important Questions*

Question #1: Who should own the life insurance?

If a client is the owner of a life insurance policy, he or she has control over the policy, and, as a result, the proceeds of the policy are includable in the client's taxable estate for estate tax purposes. Therefore, in order to avoid taxation, a life insurance policy purchased to pay estate tax *should not be owned by the client*, but rather by:

- The client's children, or

- An Irrevocable Life Insurance Trust (ILIT), over which the client has no control.

If the client's children own the policy, the client typically gifts the premium to the children every year, and they, in turn, forward payment to the insurance company. If the policy is owned by an ILIT, the client pays the premium to the trustee of the ILIT, and the trustee pays the insurance company (see "Crummey letters," below).

In choosing whether to have the children or an ILIT own the life insurance policy, clients should take into account the children's ages and the risk that a child may get divorced, sued, or file bankruptcy. If a client chooses to have the children be the owners, I often recommend, for example, that the children purchase umbrella policies on their homeowner and automobile insurance policies. Doing this reduces at least a portion of the risk. Clearly, however, the advantages and disadvantages of child ownership vs. an ILIT must be taken into account in each individual situation.

For estate planning purposes, many married couples purchase a "second-to-die" insurance policy, the proceeds of which are paid out upon the second death, when the federal estate tax is due. Because the insurance industry calculates that two people live longer than one, the premiums on a second-to-die policy are typically significantly lower than if either the husband or wife purchased a policy on his or her individual life. In the absence of extenuating circumstances, these policies should also be owned by the children or an ILIT.

Question #2: What are Crummey Letters?

When a client pays a life insurance premium to the trustee of an ILIT, he or she typically wants the payment to qualify for the annual gift tax exclusion (i.e., $13,000 per donee, or $26,000 per donee for a married couple). In order to give the ILIT beneficiaries a "present interest" in the premium payments (which is necessary for the premium payments to qualify for the annual exclusion), the trustee must send letters, known as "Crummey letters" (so named because the family who tested the law was named Crummey) to each ILIT beneficiary. The letters give the beneficiaries a certain period of time (usually 30 days) to withdraw a specified amount of the premium paid into the ILIT. (Figure 8)

Question #3: Which ILIT beneficiaries are entitled to receive Crummey Letters?

The ILIT document specifies which beneficiaries are entitled to receive Crummey letters. It's fair to assume that clients want all (or as much as possible) of the premium paid into an ILIT to qualify for the

CRUMMEY LETTERS

The trustee of the ILIT sends Crummey letters to the beneficiaries so that they have a "present interest" in the ILIT, which is required for the premium payments to qualify for the annual gift tax exclusion.

Figure 8

annual gift tax exclusion. Therefore, particularly with large premiums, clients want to maximize the number of Crummey beneficiaries. Grandchildren can be included as Crummey letter recipients, even if their rights to receive a share of the ILIT are contingent on a parent's predeceasing the client. (See *Estate of Cristofani v. Commissioner*).

Question #4: How much of each premium paid into an ILIT is a Crummey Letter recipient entitled to withdraw?

Again, the terms of the ILIT will control this. Typically, however, even though the annual gift tax exclusion is $13,000 per client (or $26,000 for a married couple), per beneficiary, each Crummey letter recipient is limited, where possible, to withdrawing no more than:

- $5,000, or

- 5% of the ILIT principal.

This is referred to as the "5&5" rule. If a Crummey beneficiary is authorized to withdraw more than the $5,000 or 5%, he or she may face certain adverse gift tax consequences. This is known as the "excess lapse problem."

Often, with a large policy, it's not possible to limit each Crummey beneficiary's withdrawal right to $5,000 or 5%, and still cover the entire premium amount. In such a case, the ILIT may be drafted to include "hanging powers," testamentary powers of appointment, or separate beneficial shares. Alternatively, the client may opt to simply use up a portion of his or her federal estate tax exclusion to the extent the annual premium contributed to the ILIT exceeds the total of all available 5&5 withdrawal rights. He or she would have to file a gift tax return, but no tax would be due to the extent that the $1,000,000 lifetime gifting cap is not exceeded.

Let's look at an example. A few months ago, I met with a married couple, the "Does," who wanted to buy a $2,000,000 second-to-die life insurance policy to pay federal estate tax. They have three children and one grandchild. After discussions with the client, the life insurance agent, Troy, and I recommended that the policy be owned by an ILIT. The annual premium payments were expected to be approximately $18,000. I suggested that the three children be the ILIT beneficiaries, with a provision that, if a child were to predecease his or her parents, that child's share would go to his or her children (i.e., a *per stirpes* distribution).

When I went to draft the ILIT, I had to figure the best way to structure the Crummey withdrawal powers for gift tax purposes. Ultimately, I decided to grant Crummey withdrawal powers to the three children and any living grandchildren. I knew that, if possible, I wanted to restrict each Crummey beneficiary withdrawal right to $5,000 or less, in order to avoid the "excess lapse" problem. If I included only the three children, I would have had to give each child an annual withdrawal right of $6,000.

By granting withdrawal powers to the three children and the living grandchild, each beneficiary would have the right to withdraw only $4,500. (Figure 9)

Thus, by maximizing the number of Crummey beneficiaries, I avoided the excess lapse problem.

Question #5: Can the client pay the premium directly to the insurance company if the policy is owned by the children or an ILIT?

Yes, the client can pay the life insurance premium directly to the insurance company without triggering inclusion of the proceeds in the client's taxable estate. It is rarely done, however, because the premium payments do not qualify for the annual gift tax exclusion. Although no gift tax is due, each year the client has to file a gift tax return, reporting that he or she has used up a portion of his or her federal estate tax exclusion.

Years ago, I had a client who didn't want his children to know he had an ILIT. He opted to pay the premium directly to the insurance company, so that Crummey letters wouldn't have to be sent to the children. In his mind, the ability to keep the policy a secret outweighed the gift tax consequences.

Question #6: What if ownership of an existing life insurance policy is transferred to the children or an ILIT?

If an existing life insurance policy is transferred to the children or an ILIT, two issues arise. First, the

AVOIDING THE "EXCESS LAPSE" PROBLEM

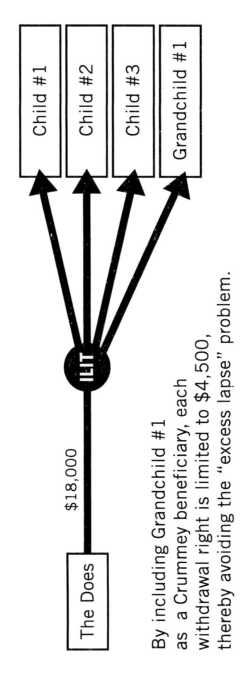

The Does — $18,000 → ILIT → Child #1, Child #2, Child #3, Grandchild #1

By including Grandchild #1 as a Crummey beneficiary, each withdrawal right is limited to $4,500, thereby avoiding the "excess lapse" problem.

Figure 9

transfer is deemed to be a gift to the children or the ILIT beneficiaries in an amount generally equal to the cash value of the policy. Technically, the amount gifted is equal to the "interpolated terminal reserve." (Simple, isn't it?!) With an ILIT, Crummey letters must be sent in order for the transfer to qualify for the gift tax annual exclusion.

Second, when an existing life insurance policy is transferred to the children or an ILIT, there is a three-year "look-back" period. That means that if the client dies within three years of the transfer, the policy's death benefit will be pulled back into the client's gross estate, and therefore subject to federal estate tax. By contrast, a new policy initially applied for by the children or the trustee of the ILIT has no such "look-back" risk. It immediately avoids federal estate tax.

◆ Charitable Remainder Trust with Wealth Replacement Trust

Clients can set up a charitable remainder trust (CRT) to reduce federal estate tax liability. Although there are a variety of forms of CRTs, and a number of specialized tax rules that apply to these trusts, here are the basics.

When a CRT is established, there is an exchange of promises. The client agrees to transfer what remains in the CRT to a charity or charities when the CRT terminates, which is at the end of a specified lifetime, or lifetimes (presumably the client's lifetime, but possibly including the spouse's and/or children's lifetimes as well), or at the end of a certain term of years. In exchange, the trustee of the CRT agrees to distribute a stream of income back to the client (and to the spouse and/or children after the client passes away, if that is how the client chose to draft the CRT) each year until the CRT terminates.

The income stream must be at least 5%, but, in my experience, is typically 6–8%. When assets are transferred into a CRT, the client avoids the capital gains tax that would have been paid if he or she had sold the assets. The CRT can sell the assets without capital gain liability because the CRT is for the ultimate benefit of a charity. In addition, the client is entitled to a significant income tax charitable deduction, which can be carried forward five years, if necessary. Finally, assets in the CRT avoid estate tax upon the client's death.

When the client dies, however, the children are likely to be upset because they will not receive any of the assets originally transferred into the CRT. In many cases, however, the client uses some portion of the income stream he or she receives annually from the CRT to buy a life insurance policy on his or her life (or a second-to-die policy for a married couple) within an ILIT (i.e., a "wealth replacement trust") in the amount of the assets contributed to the CRT. In that case, the children will typically be better off than if the CRT had never been established, because the proceeds from the life insurance policy will pass to them income and estate tax free. (Figure 10)

CHARITABLE REMAINDER TRUST

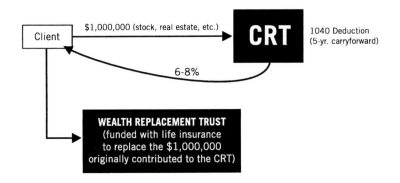

Figure 10

◆ Testamentary Charitable Lead Trust

Testamentary charitable lead trusts (CLTs) have become very popular in my practice in the wake of EG-TRRA. As mentioned previously, the federal estate tax exclusion, though relatively high in 2009, and unlimited in 2010, is schedule to drop dramatically in 2011. In this uncertain tax environment, many clients are looking for a vehicle that will serve as a "bobber," allowing their estate planning to rise and fall with the exclusion over time. The testamentary charitable lead trust is a good solution.

A CLT is often referred to as the "mirror image" of a CRT. Assets are put in the CLT, and the income from the CLT goes to a charity or charities for a term of years. At the end of the term, whatever assets remain in the CLT return to the children (or other named beneficiaries), estate tax free.

Many clients have set up their estate planning documents so that the "then available federal estate tax exclusion amount" is left to their children, with the remainder to a CLT. The CLT only comes into effect, therefore, upon the client's death, and only to the extent the client's assets exceed the federal estate tax exclusion. The terms of the CLT could provide, for example, that the income from assets in the CLT would go to charity for 20 years, and at the end of the 20-year term, the assets remaining in the CLT would pass to the children, or even to a trust for the ongoing benefit of all of the client's present and future descendants (i.e., a "dynasty trust"). In addition, if it is important to the client, the CLT could be set up so that the 20-year income stream would be payable to a family foundation or donor-directed fund established by the client. (Figure 11)

TESTAMENTARY CHARITABLE LEAD TRUST

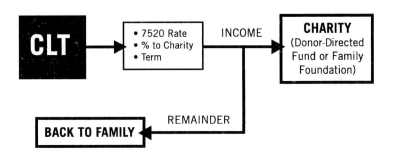

Figure 11

Finally, it doesn't hurt to tell clients that Jacqueline Onassis had a CLT. Who doesn't want to be like American royalty? Whatever the reason clients choose to use a testamentary CLT, the estate tax savings can be significant.

◆ Family Limited Partnership

A family limited partnership (FLP) is made up of general and limited partnership interests. The general partner(s) has some control of the assets in the FLP and the right to charge a management fee. The limited partners have an ownership interest, but limited control. The goal is for clients to transfer most of the value of the FLP to their children (or other beneficiaries) via gifts. The IRS allows the client to apply lack of marketability and minority interest discounts to the gifts. (Figure 12)

FAMILY LIMITED PARTNERSHIP

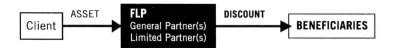

ADVANTAGES
1. Control
2. Discounted Gifting
3. Creditor Protection (beneficiaries)

Figure 12

In theory, FLPs allow clients to transfer most of the value of an asset to their children (or other beneficiaries) through discounted gifts, while still retaining some control of the asset and the right to receive income.

FLPs have come under heightened IRS scrutiny in recent years, however. The IRS has been successful not only in denying deep gifting discounts, but also in pulling the entire value of the gifted FLP interests back into the client's federal taxable estate at death. In setting up an FLP, it is extremely important that you and your clients work with an experienced estate planning attorney.

◆ Limited Liability Company

Limited liability companies (LLCs) are very similar to FLPs, and are used to transfer assets to children (or other beneficiaries) at discounted values, while allowing the client to retain some control and receive some of the income generated by the asset.

◆ Qualified Personal Residence Trust

A primary residence or second home can be transferred to the children (or other beneficiaries) at a discounted value through a qualified personal residence trust (QPRT). The client retains the right to use the property for a term of years, and then, at the end of that term, can enter into a long-term lease of the property. (Figure 13)

There is a downside to the use of a QPRT, however. If the client dies during the term of years specified in the

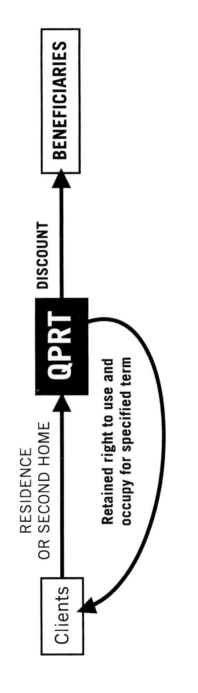

QUALIFIED PERSONAL RESIDENCE TRUST

BENEFICIARIES

DISCOUNT

QPRT

RESIDENCE
OR SECOND HOME

Retained right to use and
occupy for specified term

Clients

Figure 13

QPRT, some portion of the full date of death value of the real estate is includable in the client's taxable estate for estate tax purposes.

◆ Grantor Retained Annuity Trust

A client can gift assets at a discount, with a retained income stream, through a grantor retained annuity trust (GRAT). In addition to the leveraged gifting advantage of a GRAT, all future appreciation in the asset inside the GRAT is transferred to the GRAT beneficiaries.

As with a QPRT, the downside to a GRAT is that some portion of the full value of the assets in the GRAT is includable in the client's federal taxable estate if the client dies during the GRAT term. (Figure 14)

GRANTOR RETAINED ANNUITY TRUST

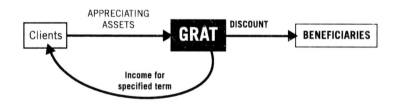

Figure 14

◆ Intentionally Defective Irrevocable Trust

Sale of closely-held stock to an intentionally defective irrevocable trust (IDIT) is a valuable estate planning tool. IDIT planning allows a client to pass on most of the value of his or her closely-held corporation to his or her children, while still maintaining maximum control, by:

1) Recapitalizing the stock into voting and non-voting shares;

2) Structuring the IDIT as a "grantor trust" for income tax purposes (i.e., the grantor is treated as the trust owner for income tax purposes);

3) Including dynasty trust provisions in the IDIT so that the trust will be for the ongoing benefit of the client's children and more remote descendants;

4) Contributing "seed money" (usually 10%) to the IDIT; and

5) Selling the discounted non-voting shares to the IDIT pursuant to an arms-length agreement represented by a promissory note, with interest at the applicable federal rate (AFR). The sale between the client and the IDIT is "disregarded" for income tax purposes. See Rev. Rul. 85-13.

IDITs are particularly valuable estate planning tools because they allow for:

- Discounted gifting;

- Income tax shifting (due to "grantor trust" status);

- Estate "freezing;" (unlike a GRAT, the grantor does not need to survive the term of the promissory note to achieve tax benefit. It's extremely important, however, that the sale to the IDIT be drafted with the requisite formalities such that the value of the stock in the IDIT is not pulled back into the client's federal taxable estate at death under IRC Sec. 2036);

- Leveraging of interest rate spreads (AFR vs. the rate of return on the stock owned by the IDIT: a portion of the difference can be used to pay premiums on a life insurance policy owned by the IDIT); and

- Allocation of generation-skipping tax (GST) exemption up front (compare with a GRAT, where GST exemption cannot be allocated until the end of the retained annuity term).

Suppose, for example, Client owns a subchapter S corporation valued at $5M. He wants to get stock to his children in order to reduce his federal taxable estate, but also wants to maintain maximum control.

He faces a $1M lifetime gifting cap, in addition to the annual gift tax exclusion, so gifting is not a viable option to reduce estate tax.

He could set up an ILIT and gift the premium amount to the trustee each year, but does not have enough Crummey beneficiaries to support the large life insurance policy he would need to cover the projected federal estate tax.

He could consider premium financing, or a GRAT, but another, and often better, solution would be an IDIT.

Client could recapitalize the stock into 10% voting and 90% non-voting shares, keep the voting shares, and sell the non-voting shares, at a discount (for lack of marketability and lack of control) to an IDIT, with interest based on the AFR rate. A portion of the difference between the rate of return on the stock owned by the IDIT and the interest on the promissory note could be used to pay premiums on a life insurance policy purchased by the IDIT on Client's life (or a second-to-die policy with wife). (Figure 15)

INTENTIONALLY DEFECTIVE IRREVOCABLE TRUST

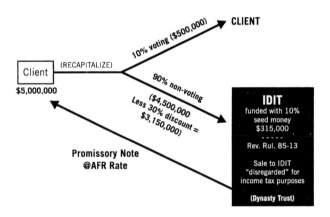

Figure 15

♦ **Conservation Easements**

Clients can place a conservation easement on their real estate, limiting future development. As a result, when the client dies, the value of the real estate is substantially reduced for estate tax purposes. This is especially suitable for family farms and substantial tracts of undeveloped land.

➤ Tax #2: State Death Tax

Historically, many states collected a portion of what was paid by a resident in federal estate tax. In the wake of EGTRRA, however, many states have enacted their own death tax statutes. Many of the statutes set the state tax exclusion amount lower than the federal estate tax exclusion, which, in some states, can trigger a state death tax upon the death of the first spouse.

Keep in mind that state death tax applies not only in the state where a client resides, but also for any state in which the client owns real estate.

State death tax can be insidious and very expensive—don't lose sight of it!

➤ Tax #3: Capital Gains Tax

Currently, when a client dies, his or her assets (with certain exceptions) get a "step-up" in basis as of the date of death. Beginning in 2010, however, step-up in tax basis will be limited. In that year only, the income tax basis of a decedent's property can increase by $1,300,000, and the income tax basis of assets passing to a surviving spouse can increase by an additional $3,000,000. A "sunset" provision restores the current full step-up in basis effective 2011. In 2010, the limitation on the step-up in tax basis is the trade-off for elimination of federal estate tax.

In my experience, the IRS doesn't do things to be kind. It expects to collect significantly more revenue from the limit on the step-up in basis—much more than it expects to lose from the elimination of the estate tax. This means clients will have an even greater need for liquidity at death. More than ever, cash will be king.

➤ Tax #4: Income Tax

● *Income in Respect of a Decedent (IRD)*

Most retirement accounts do not get a step-up in basis at death. They are subject to ordinary income tax, referred to as "IRD," or "income in respect of a decedent."

For decades, clients have contributed aggressively to their retirement accounts due to the fact that the money in the plans grows tax deferred. Over the years, those plans have grown significantly, and now often represent a substantial portion, if not most, of many clients' total net worth.

While the tax-deferred nature of retirement accounts unquestionably fuels growth, it also poses a significant planning challenge: how to avoid crushing taxation after the account owner's death. Many clients are astonished to learn that as little as 20–30% of the value of their retirement benefits may pass to their beneficiaries upon their death, after payment of federal estate tax, state death tax, generation-skipping tax, and income tax. (Figure 16)

The concepts involved with retirement plan distributions are confusing and complex. I have included the following case study, entitled "The Retirement Blues," as a

RETIREMENT ACCOUNT TAXATION

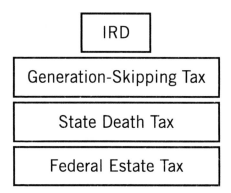

Figure 16

framework within which to highlight and discuss those concepts.

- ● **Case Study: "The Retirement Blues"**

John and Mary Retirees meet with their attorney to do some estate planning. They have the following assets:

John	Mary
800,000 Traditional IRA	600,000 Traditional IRA
1,000,000 stocks (non tax-deferred)	800,000 house
2,000,000 insurance	1,600,000 stocks (non tax-deferred)
$3,800,000 Total	$3,000,000 Total

John is a retired pilot. He turned 68 last month. Mary volunteers at the Red Cross, and is approaching her 65th birthday. They have two sons (ages 45 and 35) and four grandchildren. Some of their friends have been talking about required minimum distributions from their retirement plans, and the Retirees are concerned about what, if anything, they should be doing.

Until recently, John had his estate listed as beneficiary on his IRA. Now Mary is listed as primary beneficiary, and his two sons are equal contingent beneficiaries. Mary has listed the Red Cross as beneficiary of the first $20,000 of her IRA. The remainder will pass equally to her two sons.

What should the attorney tell the Retirees?

First, the attorney should tell the Retirees the good news. Retirement accounts are similar to life insurance and annuities. They are "beneficiary designated" assets, and therefore not subject to probate. If an individual (or charity) is listed as beneficiary, the terms of the account owner's Will or Revocable Trust will not control who receives the account benefits at the time of his or her death.

Next, the attorney should warn the Retirees. Typically, retirement plan beneficiary designation forms only give clients a small space to fill in marked "Primary Beneficiary," and another small space to fill in marked "Contingent Beneficiary." When compared to the 20–30 page Will or Revocable Trust that controls distribution of other assets such as real estate, non-tax-deferred investments, business interests and personal property, the space provided on the beneficiary designation form is insufficient for those clients with sizeable retirement accounts who may want to do some detailed beneficiary planning for those accounts. In a moment, I will suggest certain more sophisticated ways for clients to handle beneficiary designations for retirement benefits. But first, I want to take a closer look at the impact of federal estate tax and income tax on retirement benefits.

As noted above, one reason that as little as 20–30% of retirement benefits may pass to the designated beneficiary(ies) is federal estate tax. There is a very common misconception that retirement benefits are not subject to federal estate tax because they do not go through probate. *Even though they are non-probate assets, retirement benefits are subject to federal estate tax.*

Another reason that as little as 20–30% of retirement benefits may pass to the designated beneficiary(ies) is federal income tax. The technical name for the income tax due on retirement benefits is "IRD."

Unfortunately, many people think IRD means:

"**I R**eally **D**on't…know what it means."

"**I R**eally **D**on't…care."

And worst of all:

"**I R**eally **D**on't…think I'll pay any attention to it."

They are asking for trouble.

In actuality, IRD stands for "income in respect of a decedent." It is a fancy way of saying that when a person dies, he or she is is still responsible for all of the income tax that has never been paid on tax-deferred retirement plans.

Three important considerations must be taken into account regarding IRD. First, IRD is triggered by post-death distributions from a retirement account. As a result, to the extent distributions can be postponed after the account owner dies, IRD will be deferred. Second, all retirement account distributions are included in the recipient's gross income as IRD. It is therefore the distribution recipient, not the account owner's estate, who pays the income tax due. Third, the distribution recipient may claim an income tax deduction for the incremental federal estate tax paid on the IRD. This IRD deduction provides relief from the double taxation of estate and income taxes, but does not reduce the overall tax bill as much as if the income tax had not been due at all.

A solution to the IRD problem, therefore, is to figure out the best way to postpone payment of the income tax as long as possible. This is accomplished by what is commonly referred to as "stretch" planning. With stretch planning, plan owners choose those beneficiaries who can defer the income tax the longest upon the plan owner's death.

I have a few clients each year who ask me where they can buy a "stretch IRA." They are surprised when I tell them it isn't a product they purchase, but rather a planning opportunity that defers the income tax due on their retirement accounts.

Typically, the surviving spouse can defer the income tax the longest for three reasons. First, a surviving spouse is the only beneficiary who can roll a retirement account over into his or her own IRA, and continue deferral on the income tax. Second, unlike all other beneficiaries who must begin withdrawals immediately upon the account owner's death, a surviving spouse does not have to begin withdrawing from the rollover account until he or she turns 70½. Third, at the time of the rollover, a surviving spouse can name his or her own beneficiaries, thereby extending the income tax deferral even further upon his or her death. (Figure 17)

MAXIMUM DEFERRAL

SURVIVING SPOUSE is typically the best beneficiary *(other than charity, which escapes all taxation)*, because:

1. Spouse can defer withdrawals until 70½

2. Spouse can roll the retirement benefits into an IRA in his or her own name

3. Spouse can name new beneficiaries, making "stretch" longer

---

Figure 17

The age of 70½ is important with respect to a surviving spouse, and all retirement plan owners, because the IRS requires individuals to begin withdrawing from their retirement accounts by a certain date, known as the "required beginning date," or "RBD." With limited exception, a person's RBD is April 1st of the calendar year after he or she turns 70½. For example, suppose John turns 70 on January 1, 2008. His RBD would be April 1, 2009. If John fails to start taking his required minimum distributions on his RBD, he will be subject to a 50% IRS penalty.

On April 16, 2002, the IRS issued final regulations governing the calculation of required annual minimum distributions. The final regulations are very favorable for almost all IRA and qualified plan participants, and greatly simplify the calculation of annual lifetime minimum distributions. Under the final regulations, the beneficiary designated at the time of the account owner's RBD no longer affects the calculation of the lifetime required minimum distribution. In addition, account owners no longer need to wrestle with the recalculation election. Instead, the IRS has provided a Uniform Table, based on updated life expectancy tables, to calculate required annual lifetime minimum distributions, as shown on the next page:

Age of the Employee	Distribution Period	Applicable Percentage
70	27.4	3.6496 %
71	26.5	3.7736 %
72	25.6	3.9063 %
73	24.7	4.0486 %
74	23.8	4.2017 %
75	22.9	4.3668 %
76	22.0	4.5455 %
77	21.2	4.7170 %
78	20.3	4.9261 %
79	19.5	5.1282 %
80	18.7	5.3476 %
81	17.9	5.5866 %
82	17.1	5.8480 %
83	16.3	6.1350 %
84	15.5	6.4516 %
85	14.8	6.7568 %
86	14.1	7.0922 %
87	13.4	7.4627 %
88	12.7	7.8740 %
89	12.0	8.3333 %
90	11.4	8.7719 %
91	10.8	9.2593 %
92	10.2	9.8039 %
93	9.6	10.4167 %
94	9.1	10.9890 %
95	8.6	11.6279 %
96	8.1	12.3457 %
97	7.5	13.1579 %
98	7.1	14.0845 %
99	6.7	14.9254 %
100	6.3	15.8730 %
101	5.9	16.9492 %
102	5.5	18.1818 %
103	5.2	19.2308 %
104	4.9	20.4082 %
105	4.6	22.2222 %
106	4.2	23.8095 %
107	3.9	25.6410 %
108	3.7	27.0270 %
109	3.4	29.4118 %
110	3.1	32.2581 %
111	2.9	34.4828 %
112	2.6	38.4615 %
113	2.4	41.6667 %
114	2.1	47.6190 %
115 and older	1.9	52.6316 %

The Uniform Table assumes that all designated beneficiaries are ten years younger than the taxpayer, and their joint life expectancies are recalculated every year. There is only one exception. If a spouse is designated as beneficiary, and if the spouse is more than ten years younger than the account owner, the couple's actual joint life expectancy can be used to determine required lifetime minimum distributions.

The final regulations also contain more favorable rules for calculation of post-death required minimum distributions. The major change is that, under the new regulations, the designated beneficiary is determined as of September 30th of the calendar year following the account owner's date of death (the "Beneficiary Determination Date"). The result is that there is a "shake-out period," from the date of death to September 30th of the following calendar year, during which valuable postmortem "stretch" planning can occur. Specifically, the "shake-out period" allows for:

a. Creation of separate accounts;

b. Cashing out of improper beneficiaries (the IRS, for technical reasons, defines improper beneficiaries to include charities. This is ironic, because *retirement accounts should always, to the extent possible, be used for charitable bequests.* Anything left to charity from a retirement account avoids *all taxation*, including estate tax and IRD).

c. Disclaimers

These three options are discussed below. (Figure 18)

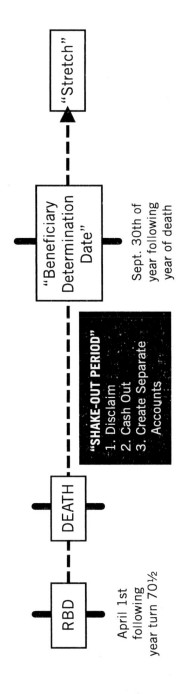

NEW TIMELINE

RBD	April 1st following year turn 70½
DEATH	
	"SHAKE-OUT PERIOD" 1. Disclaim 2. Cash Out 3. Create Separate Accounts
"Beneficiary Determination Date"	Sept. 30th of year following year of death
"Stretch"	

Figure 18

But first, let's go back to our case study. John had at one point named his estate as beneficiary of his IRA. Unfortunately, I see this all too often, with the same disastrous results.

NEVER LIST A CLIENT'S ESTATE AS THE BENEFICIARY OF RETIREMENT ACCOUNTS!!!

The final regulations confirm that, when a person names his or her estate as beneficiary of his or her retirement benefits, he or she is deemed not to have a designated beneficiary, and all of the income tax due on the retirement account must be paid within the shortest period allowed by law: (i) within five years if the account owner dies before his or her RBD, or (ii) over the remaining actuarial life expectancy of the account owner, if he or she dies after his or her RBD. Income tax deferral is completely thwarted. Fortunately, John changed his beneficiary from his estate to Mary, so Mary can take advantage of the spousal rollover upon John's death.

Suppose in our case study that John decides to leave his IRA to his two sons, who are ten years apart in age. Is this good planning? Yes and no. Yes, the retirement benefits will go to the people John intended; but no, Mary will not be able to take advantage of the spousal rollover. Assuming John has an independent reason to list his two sons, as opposed to Mary, as primary beneficiaries, under the new regulations, he has done the right thing. As outlined above, the final regulations determine the designated beneficiary(ies) for post-mortem minimum distributions as of September 30th of the calendar year following the date of death. As a result, as long as separate accounts are created for John's two sons as of the Beneficiary Determination Date, each son can use his own life expectancy in calculating post-death minimum distributions.

Under the old rules, designation of the two sons would have been problematic. The rules specified that when more than one person was named as beneficiary on a retirement account, the oldest beneficiary's life expectancy determined the maximum deferral of the income tax. Because younger beneficiaries had to withdraw their shares based on the oldest beneficiary's life expectancy, they were forced to pay income tax much sooner than if they had been able to take withdrawals over their own life expectancies. John's younger son would have had to take his withdrawals ten years earlier than necessary. Under the old rules, the only exception would have been if John had created separate accounts as of his RBD, or if John had died before his RBD and the sons created separate accounts before the end of the calendar year of John's death. Comparing the new rules with the old, we see the opportunity for, and value of, post-mortem planning prior to the Beneficiary Determination Date.

It is interesting to note that, under the new regulations, if a non-spouse beneficiary dies during the period between the account owner's death and the Beneficiary Determination Date, the beneficiary will continue to be treated as the "designated beneficiary," and his or her actuarial life expectancy will be used to calculate minimum post-death distributions.

Let's continue with our case study. Mary has left the first $20,000 of her IRA to the Red Cross and the remainder to her two sons. Again, assuming Mary has an independent reason to forego the spousal rollover, Mary's decision is appropriate under the final regulations. Upon her death, the designated beneficiary(ies) for post-mortem minimum distributions will be determined as of September 30th of the calendar year following her date of death. As a result, as long as (i) the charitable bequest of $20,000 to the Red Cross is cashed out prior to the Beneficiary Determination Date, and (ii) separate accounts are created for the two sons prior to the Beneficiary Determination Date, each son should then be able to use his own life expectancy in calculating post-mortem minimum distributions on the remaining IRA balance. I would like to add a word of caution, however, in light of certain issues raised recently by the IRS. In order to be certain to preserve the "stretch" for the two sons, rather than naming the Red Cross and the two sons as beneficiaries on the same IRA, it may be advisable for Mary to create two separate IRA accounts during her lifetime. She could put $20,000 in IRA #1, and designate the Red Cross as beneficiary; and she could put the remaining $580,000 (of her original $600,000 IRA) in IRA #2, and designate the two sons as beneficiaries.

Under the old rules, designation of the Red Cross and the two sons as beneficiaries would have been a disaster. If a person named a charity as beneficiary of part of a group of beneficiaries of a retirement plan, they were deemed to have no designated beneficiary, and the opportunity for "stretch" planning was lost. The $20,000 charitable bequest would have forced Mary's two sons to pay the income tax on their shares of Mary's IRA much sooner than necessary after her death. They would have lost the ability to defer the IRD. Again, comparing the new rules with the old, we see the value of post-mortem planning during the "shake-out period."

Many clients ask whether a trust can be named as beneficiary of a retirement account. In the past, it was difficult to name a trust as beneficiary, but the new regulations recognize a trust as a valid designated beneficiary if:

i)   the trust is valid under state law,

ii)   the trust is, or will become, irrevocable on the death of the account owner,

iii) the beneficiaries of the trust are identifiable from the trust instrument, and

iv) a copy of the trust agreement or a certification of beneficiaries is provided to the plan administrator by October 31st of the year following the year of the account owner's death.

Generally, if a trust is designated as beneficiary, post-death minimum required distributions must begin the year following the account owner's death, and are calculated based on the life expectancy of the oldest trust beneficiary. There are complicated rules governing the designation of a trust as beneficiary of a retirement account, however, particularly with respect to application of the "separate account" rule to testamentary trusts (e.g., "Ferrari" trusts, special needs trusts, etc.). It is crucial that you work with an estate planning attorney who understands, and keeps abreast of the changes in, this complex area of the law.

Perhaps the most notable trend in distribution of retirement benefits is the increased use of disclaimer planning in beneficiary designations. A disclaimer is a beneficiary's refusal to accept something that has been left to him or her. For a disclaimer to be effective, (i) it must be exercised in writing, (ii) with limited exception, it must be made within nine months of the account holder's death, and (iii) the person disclaiming can not have accepted any of the disclaimed asset or any interest therein, exerted any control over the disclaimed asset, accepted a benefit from it, or have waived his or her right to disclaim. (Note that the technical requirements to make a valid disclaimer vary from state to state, and a disclaimer should always be made with the assistance of legal counsel.)

Disclaimers are crucial because they allow clients to build flexibility into their retirement benefit planning. If the beneficiary of a retirement account disclaims his or her interest, the law treats the situation as if the beneficiary had predeceased the account owner. In that case, the retirement asset passes to the contingent beneficiary.

I find that disclaimer planning is particularly useful where retirement accounts represent a substantial portion of a couple's total net worth. In our case study, for example, John's IRA is worth $800,000, and his other assets are worth $3,000,000. For "stretch" purposes, it would be best if John named Mary as beneficiary on his IRA because she could take advantage of the spousal rollover, and defer the income tax. However, if John leaves the

$800,000 IRA to Mary outright, upon his death, Mary's assets will be worth $3,800,000 (i.e., John's $800,000 IRA rolled over into Mary's name, plus the $3,000,000 originally in Mary's name). If Mary dies in 2009, she can shelter only $3,500,000 from federal estate tax upon her death, so approximately $135,000 of federal estate tax would be due when she dies. On the one hand, John wants to roll over the IRA to Mary and defer the IRD, but on the other hand, he wants to reduce federal estate tax upon Mary's death.

The best way for John to balance these competing tax interests is for him to incorporate disclaimer planning into his beneficiary designation. He could list Mary as the primary beneficiary of his IRA, but provide that if Mary disclaims (i.e., says she does not want) all or some portion of John's $800,000 IRA, then the disclaimed amount will go to John's credit shelter trust. His credit shelter trust is set up to hold up to $3,500,000 (i.e., John's federal estate tax exclusion until 2009) for Mary's benefit during her lifetime. Any money left in the credit shelter trust when Mary dies passes to John's two sons, federal estate tax free. (Figure 19)

If John's IRA beneficiary designation is set up this way, when John dies, Mary will have complete flexibility to decide which tax advantage is most beneficial to her. She can decide at that time whether it is better for her to (i) roll the IRA over into her own name and defer the IRD, or (ii) disclaim all or some portion of the IRA into John's credit shelter trust and avoid estate tax upon her death. The federal estate tax rate is higher than the federal in-

DISCLAIMER PLANNING
WITH RETIREMENT BENEFITS

Maximum IRD Deferral	vs.	Maximum use of Estate Tax Exclusion

Total Estate Tax Exclusion:	**$3,500,000**
John's Other Assets:	**$3,000,000**
Needed to Fill Up Exclusion:	**$500,000**

John's IRA:	**$800,000**
Mary Takes:	**$300,000**
Credit Shelter Trust:	**$500,000**

Figure 19

come tax rate, so it is often best for a spouse to disclaim and have all or some portion of the IRA go to the credit shelter trust.

Suppose, however, that John is worried that Mary may not disclaim, even if federal estate tax would be avoided. Suppose he is afraid she may remarry and leave the retirement account to her new spouse (Remember our friend, "Sven The Tennis Pro"?). In that case, John could list his credit shelter trust as primary beneficiary of his IRA, and provide that any amount disclaimed would pass either to Mary outright, or to a marital (i.e., QTIP) trust for Mary's benefit during her lifetime. If John names a professional, disinterested trustee of his credit shelter trust, that trustee can determine how much of the IRA needs to go into John's credit shelter trust to take advantage of his federal estate tax exclusion, and how much should be disclaimed and pass to Mary or the marital trust. One advantage of naming the marital trust is that it allows Mary to use the money as long as she is alive, but upon her death, whatever remains in the marital trust passes to John's two sons.

➤ Tax #5: Generation-Skipping Tax

The IRS wants to impose a federal gift or estate tax on each generation. As a result, if a transfer is made, outright or in trust, to a beneficiary two or more generations younger than the person making the transfer (i.e., a "skip person"), the IRS counts on the generation-skipping tax (GST) to make up the revenue lost by not being able to tax the intervening generation.

The GST rate is equal to the highest federal estate tax rate, and is imposed in addition to the federal gift and estate tax. Many practitioners are under the misconception that the GST applies only if a client is gifting or bequeathing something directly to a grandchild or more remote descendant. The GST casts a broad net, however, and is extremely complex. It applies to many other situations as well. For example, the GST applies to transfers to non-family members who are more than 37½ years younger than the transferor. It can also apply to a trust set up during lifetime or at death for the benefit of a child. If such a trust is established to hold assets until the child reaches a certain age (i.e., a "Ferrari" trust), and if the assets pass to the child's children because the child dies before reaching the specified age, GST will apply.

GST can be avoided three ways. First, the GST does not apply if assets pass to a grandchild as a result of his or her parent having predeceased. This is known as the "predeceased ancestor rule." Second, each individual has a GST exemption equal to the federal estate tax exclusion. Third, certain transfers that qualify for the $13,000 annual gift tax exclusion are also exempt from GST.

Suffice it to say, GST planning is not for the faint of heart. It's important that you bring in a competent estate planning lawyer and an experienced accountant as part of your team, so that all implications of the GST are adequately addressed in the estate planning process.

■ GOAL #3: AVOID THE "MENENDEZ PROBLEM"

The ultimate purpose of estate planning for most clients is to transfer the family's assets to the children in the most advantageous way possible. Because estate planning can be complex, and because people often receive "cocktail party" advice about what should or should not be done with their assets, many children are anxious about whether their parents have adequately planned their estates. The children fear that the planning has never been done, has not been done properly, or is taking place "behind the curtain."

While the decision as to how thoroughly to inform the children about the details of the estate plan depends entirely on the family dynamics, it can be helpful to provide some general reassurance. At minimum, parents should consider (i) identifying for their children the members of the estate planning team; (ii) confirming the existence of advanced health care directives; (iii) disclosing the location of important documents; and (iv) reassuring the children that the wealth transfer has been planned for appropriately. In some cases, and especially where one or more of the children has been assigned a fiduciary role in the estate plan, it may be helpful for parents and child(ren) to meet with the attorney to discuss the child(ren)'s role and how the plan will operate. When parents do these things, it's more likely that the children will feel invested in the estate planning process and reassured that the plan will operate smoothly and to their benefit.

Of course, another way to avoid the "Menendez Problem" is for clients to pretend they're poor! I'm always amazed by how many clients choose this option.

Chapter Four

—

RULE #4

FOCUS ON CLIENT GOALS — SALES WILL FOLLOW

I have the world's best clients. Years ago, one of them sent me a cartoon. There was a picture of a woman in her 90's shaking her finger violently at her husband. The caption read, "I don't care what our estate planning lawyer says, I'm not having another baby!"

I've always loved that cartoon for two reasons. First, there are very few estate planning jokes. What's more, it's a good one. Second, and more important, the cartoon perfectly captures Rule #4. All too often, when working with an estate planning client, the financial professional works in reverse. He or she starts by focusing on the solution—the sale—and then works backward to fit that sale into the client's situation. Nothing, let me repeat, **nothing**, will prompt me to remove an advisor from my team faster, or more permanently. Without exception, the client's individual needs must dictate estate planning recommendations. Surprisingly, once you recognize and live by this rule, sales typically follow, with the endorsement of the other team members.

We often joke in our office about an investment advisor who didn't abide by Rule #4. He and I had a few mutual clients, each with very different asset profiles. Each time we discussed his recommendation for a particular client, however, he said the client needed a $1,000,000 insurance policy. This was true regardless of whether the client had assets valued at $500,000 or $7,000,000. In the office, we refer to him as the "one-trick pony." He's a perfect example of a financial advisor who worked in reverse. I concluded that he recommended $1,000,000 of insurance to everyone, regardless of the facts, the clients' estate planning goals, or the clients' financial needs. Needless to say, after recognizing that he used the same financial "analysis" with every client, we opted out of working with him. We knew he wasn't focused on his clients' best interests.

There's another advisor who comes to mind with respect to Rule #4. He's a legend in our office. For purposes of this discussion, I'll call him "I'm Just a Numbers Guy."

"I'm Just a Numbers Guy" was spanking new to the business. It was his first month in town. He had heard our firm's name associated with estate planning, so he invited David and me to lunch. It was a very short lunch. David actually walked out, which was a first. Suffice it to say, "I'm Just a Numbers Guy" had no intention of focusing on client need. He had it all figured out another way—mathematically. He calculated that if he cold-called enough people to get 16 appointments a week, four of those appointments would turn into some type of sale. He figured further that if he did that for two years, he would have 400 clients, and then could go on "auto-pilot" (his words, not mine!), just collecting his annual fees. There was no discussion of helping people. He didn't mention addressing each client's unique situation. As he, in his own words, said, "To me, it's just a numbers game." I haven't seen him since, and I understand he's no longer in the business. No big surprise (or loss!).

On the other hand, smart advisors fully appreciate that if they put client needs first, sales typically follow. Tom is a perfect example. I first met Tom about 10 years ago. He is a financial advisor, and I consider him a valuable member of my team, even though he lives and works primarily in another state. We don't work together a great deal, but when we do, I know the client is in good hands.

Here's just one example of many I could give involving Tom. He referred a client to my husband about a year ago. The client and his wife had a substantial estate, which included a closely held business. The client's son worked in the business, and the client wanted to discuss his business succession options. Tom and my husband had a number of lengthy meetings with the client, and, for a variety of reasons, they all decided it was in the client's best interest to sit tight and do nothing immediately, but to review the situation in one or two years. Tom received no compensation for his time, and made no sale.

Our office, of course, moved forward with the client's estate planning. Early in the process, we discovered records relating to 10 life insurance policies. In addition, although I found reference to an irrevocable life insurance trust (ILIT), it wasn't clear whether ownership of the 10 policies had been transferred into the ILIT, or whether the policies were even still in place.

I e-mailed Tom. He responded promptly, saying he had no knowledge of the policies, but that he believed he had heard something about a second-to-die policy the client and his wife had purchased from someone else a year or so back. He suggested I get in touch with the client's daughter, which I did. She confirmed the existence of the second-to-die policy (the face value of which was very large), and told me she was "in charge of some trust" holding the policy, but really didn't know what her responsibilities were. She hadn't heard anything about the policy or the trust in over a year.

You can imagine my response. The first thing that flashed through my mind was, "What about the Crummey letters?!" (See Rule #3) I immediately called Tom. He got me the information I needed about the second-to-die policy so I could work effectively with the clients (and their daughter). Again, he received no remuneration, and there was no product sale.

A month or so later, the sale arrived, in the form of two long-term care policies. Although the client (apparently) had a life insurance agent, when I recommended that he purchase nursing home insurance, he said he wanted to work with Tom because Tom had shown commitment to his family's concerns and needs. The client also expressed displeasure that he hadn't heard from the other insurance agent since the original insurance was purchased. (See Rule #6!)

The story does not end there, however. The client's daughter was also very impressed with Tom and his commitment to her parents. She is an executive at a global financial company, and has expressed interest in having Tom work with her and her husband on their personal affairs. More sales will follow, all because Tom is someone who always puts client need first.

Chapter Five

—

RULE #5

EMBRACE UNCLE SAM

You've all heard the old joke: "We're from the IRS and we're here to help." I think we can all agree that this statement warrants healthy skepticism (!), but, in the world of estate planning, at least some of the time it's true.

You must not think of current tax law as cast in stone. It is, in fact, very dynamic and fluid. Many tax law changes can be used to the client's benefit. By staying abreast of these changes, you can be of service to your clients while distinguishing yourself professionally.

Here are two examples of changes in the tax law that led to estate planning opportunity in my practice:

EXAMPLE #1: EGTRRA

The Economic Growth and Tax Relief Reconciliation Act (EGTRRA) was enacted on June 7, 2001. It included important estate, gift and generation-skipping transfer-tax changes.

The most publicized change, however, was the increasing, then "sunsetting," federal estate tax exclusion.

Many financial professionals thought EGTRRA was the death knell of their careers. Some thought it was time to retire. I always saw it differently, however. I saw EGTRRA as an opportunity.

■ PLANNING FOR SECOND SPOUSES

The first people I thought of when I saw the new estate tax exclusion amounts under EGTRRA were my clients in second marriages. I realized they faced two new threats.

➤ Threat #1: Possible Disinheritance of the Second Spouse

In the past, many of my clients in second marriages opted to leave the federal estate tax exclusion amount to their children from their prior marriage. This was an effective way to ease potential tensions between the second spouse and the children, so that the children did not have to wait until the step parent died before receiving at least a portion of their inheritance.

I realized those clients needed to revisit their planning, however, in the wake of EGTRRA. As the federal estate tax exclusion rose, there would be an increasing possibility that the second spouse could be disinherited. For example, I had a client with a $2,000,000 estate. A few years ago, when the federal estate tax exclusion was $625,000, we set up his estate planning so that his children from a prior marriage would receive the amount of the estate tax exclusion, and his second spouse would receive the remainder in a QTIP Trust. After

EGTRRA, unless the client amended his estate planning documents, as of 2006 (when the estate tax exemption rose to $2,000,000), his second spouse would receive nothing. I could envision her reaction!

Ultimately, the client did amend his documents. He also set up a charitable remainder trust, naming his children as income beneficiaries upon his death.

➤ Threat #2: Possible Increased Claims Under the Elective Share

I realized that as the estate tax exclusion increased under EG-TRRA, a larger portion of a decedent's assets would pass to the credit shelter trust, to the exclusion of the QTIP trust. The credit shelter trust is typically established for the benefit of the client's surviving spouse and descendants. The QTIP trust, however, is for the sole benefit of the surviving spouse.

As credit shelter trusts grow in response to the increased death tax exclusion, spouses (particularly second spouses) may feel "cheated." They may feel they have restricted access to funds because they have to "share" the credit shelter trust with their stepchildren. The result could be an increase in claims under the spousal elective share.

By law, typically, in the absence of a prenuptial agreement to the contrary, and regardless of the express provisions in any estate planning documents, a surviving spouse is entitled to a legally designated fraction of his or her deceased spouse's estate outright upon death. The fraction is typically one-third (⅓), but varies by state. This is known as the "elective share." I recognized that it would therefore be increasingly important that clients in a second marriage have sufficient liquidity to pay out the elective share, if necessary. This was particularly true for those clients whose estates were made up primarily of real estate or closely held business interests. In such cases, their survivors could be forced to sell those illiquid assets at a distress sale in order to pay the elective share.

In the wake of EGTRRA, many of my clients in second marriages purchased life insurance in an amount to pay out the elective share, if claimed by the surviving spouse. In each case, the change in the exclusion amount under EGTRRA brought opportunity, not defeat, for both the client and the financial professionals.

■ PUTTING THE CREDIT SHELTER TRUST "ON STEROIDS"

The second thing I thought of when I saw the increasing estate tax exclusions under EGTRRA was the opportunity to put credit shelter trusts "on steroids."

As the estate tax exclusion amount (and, therefore, the amount in the credit shelter trust) goes up under EGTRRA, it is increasingly likely that the credit shelter trust beneficiaries (typically, the surviving spouse and the decedent's descendants) will not need all or some portion of the trust principal for lifetime distributions. Given that all appreciation in a credit shelter trust is exempt from tax upon the surviving spouse's death, I realized it would be beneficial if the credit shelter trust principal not needed by the beneficiaries were used to buy a life insurance policy. Upon the death of the surviving spouse, the life insurance proceeds would pass to the remaining trust beneficiaries, income and estate tax free. By comparison, if assets in the credit shelter trust were invested for growth, the beneficiaries would not reap the same income tax benefit because all appreciation occurring after the first spouse's death would be subject to capital gain.

Let me share an example from my practice where life insurance was purchased within a credit shelter trust, thereby putting the trust "on steroids."

A few months ago, a financial advisor recommended that one my clients, "Widow X," buy life insurance to pay the federal estate tax that was likely to be due upon her death. I wasn't wild about the idea for two reasons. First, Widow X only had three daughters (no grandchildren), so she would have had to use a significant portion of her federal estate tax exclusion to support the premium for the size policy she required. Second, Widow X had been gifting the maximum gift tax exclusion amount to her daughters each year, and she wanted to continue doing so.

As an alternative, I suggested that the trustee of Widow X's deceased husband's credit shelter trust use the entire $800,000 trust principal to buy a life insurance policy within the credit shelter trust, with Widow X as the insured. When Widow X died, the insurance proceeds collected by the credit shelter trust would pass to the three daughters, estate and capital gains tax free. Widow X loved the idea. Interestingly, once I suggested that the credit shelter trust be put "on steroids," Widow X's focus changed from covering her federal estate tax liability to maximizing the capital transfer to the next generation.

More often than not, the surviving spouse serves as trustee or co-trustee of the credit shelter trust. If a life insurance policy is to be purchased within the credit shelter trust, be sure the surviving spouse irrevocably resigns as trustee or co-trustee of the credit shelter trust, and that a disinterested trustee purchases the policy. If a surviving spouse, as trustee, buys the life insurance policy on his or her life within the credit shelter trust, the IRS could argue that the surviving spouse has "incidents of ownership" over the policy, and force the policy proceeds to be included in the surviving spouse's taxable estate upon death. In addition, be sure the surviving spouse irrevocably releases any limited testamentary power of appointment he or she may have over the credit shelter trust.

Clearly, the opportunity created by EGTRRA to put credit shelter trusts "on steroids" has been advantageous for life insurance agents and, more importantly, for their clients.

EXAMPLE #2: RETIREMENT ACCOUNT FINAL REGULATIONS

As discussed previously, on April 16, 2002 the IRS issued final regulations regarding minimum distributions from retirement accounts. The regulations changed how minimum distributions are calculated during the account owner's lifetime and after his or her death. The 2002 regulations require people to take less out of their retirement accounts during their lifetimes, thereby allowing greater lifetime deferral of the IRD and increased likelihood that retirement assets will pass to the account beneficiaries at death.

Because retirement assets are the most expensive assets to pass on at death, however, the final regulations guarantee an even bigger IRD problem for beneficiaries when the account owners die. This change creates an increased need for liquidity to pay the income tax upon the account owner's death. Certain advisors embraced this change from Uncle Sam. They realized that change can equal opportunity.

■ BITE THE BULLET NOW

I was particularly impressed by "Carol," an advisor who worked with me to put the new regulations to work in a creative way. I suggested to her that clients might want to consider "biting the bullet now" (BTBN) as a remedy to the IRD problem. I knew there were certain situations where it could be advantageous for a client to withdraw all or some portion of his or her retirement benefits during his or her lifetime, pay the income tax due on the withdrawal, and convert the remainder into an asset that could grow, but be exempt from federal and state estate tax, and income tax, at the time of the client's death. Specifically, I recommended BTBN be considered for clients who (i) had more assets in retirement accounts than they would ever use during their lifetime, and (ii) had "needy" beneficiaries who were likely to withdraw their share of the retirement accounts immediately upon the owner's death, thereby triggering all of the IRD.

For example, suppose Mr. Smith has a $1,000,000 traditional IRA as part of his $5,000,000 net worth. Upon his death, Mr. Smith's beneficiaries might receive only 20–30% of the $1,000,000 IRA after payment of federal and state death taxes and IRD. If, on the other hand, Mr. Smith withdraws the $1,000,000 from his IRA, pays the $400,000 income tax liability, and uses the remaining $600,000 to buy a single premium, second-to-die, variable life insurance policy inside an ILIT, his beneficiaries will most likely be much better off. Alternatively, Mr. Smith could "bite the bullet slowly."

Rather than withdrawing the full $1,000,000 from his IRA, he could take annual withdrawals in the amounts necessary to fund an installment life insurance contract.

Despite BTBN's obvious tax benefits, it has one potentially fatal flaw. Many clients, understandably, cannot get beyond the fact that they will have to write a sizeable check to the IRS on April 15th following the year the withdrawal is made from the retirement account.

There is a solution to this problem, however, and it is based on a law of physics: "For every action, there is an equal and opposite reaction." In estate planning, this means that whenever a client takes an action that triggers adverse tax consequences, the estate planning team needs to consider what further action the client can take to offset those adverse effects. I refer to this as "linked planning."

Let's go back to our prior BTBN example, where Mr. Smith withdraws $1,000,000 from his IRA, triggering a $400,000 income tax liability. One "linked planning" option would be to have Mr. Smith set up a charitable remainder trust (CRT). If he funds the CRT with low-basis stock worth $1,000,000, he will be entitled to a substantial charitable income tax deduction. That deduction, when combined with the capital gains and estate tax savings that result from use of the CRT, will significantly offset the income tax liability triggered by the BTBN.

Use of the CRT also has a downside, however. When Mr. and Mrs. Smith die, their children will not be happy that they have lost the after-tax use of the $1,000,000 put in the CRT. Again, there's a "linked planning" solution. Mr. and

Mrs. Smith could use all or some portion of the income stream they receive from the CRT to purchase a second-to-die policy in an ILIT. This type of ILIT is commonly referred to as a "wealth replacement trust." In theory, the ILIT proceeds replace the money the children would have received if the CRT had not been established. In reality, the children are often better off because the ILIT proceeds pass to them income and estate tax free.

There's one final part to the Smiths' "linked planning." I'm a firm believer that, we, as team members, should consider every tax advantage available to our clients. When Mr. and Mrs. Smith die, the proceeds of the ILIT (funded with the net proceeds from the $1,000,000 IRA withdrawal) and the wealth replacement trust (funded with a portion of the CRT income stream) will pass to their children, free of income and estate tax. Rather than distributing the proceeds outright to the children, however, the Smiths could set up the ILIT and wealth replacement trust as "dynasty" trusts. They could be drafted so that assets in the trusts will avoid federal estate and generation-skipping tax in perpetuity. (Figure 20)

A few years ago, I asked a new client, "Mrs. Jones," what she wanted to accomplish with her estate planning. She said, "I want my great-grandchildren to know my first name." Her answer intrigued me. It wasn't something I'd heard before. She was a perfect candidate for a dynasty trust.

First, I put Mrs. Jones's $1,000,000 life insurance policy into an irrevocable life insurance trust (ILIT). I drafted the ILIT for the benefit of all her living *and future* descendants, and included language authorizing the disinterested trustee to make interest-free loans to the beneficiaries. I told Mrs.

BITE THE BULLET NOW

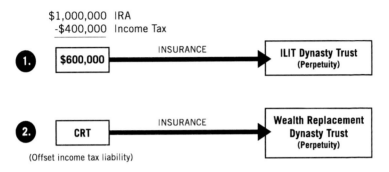

Figure 20

Jones this allowed the ILIT to be a "family bank" in perpetuity. She thought that was great.

Second, I recommended Mrs. Jones gift money each year to her daughter and grandson, so that they, in turn, could purchase a second-to-die policy within a separate dynasty ILIT. The policy proceeds would create even more cash at a later date, assuring Mrs. Jones that her legacy would continue for future generations.

Many advisors mistakenly believe that dynasty trust planning is only for the extremely wealthy. That is not the case. Increasingly, attorneys are raising it as a planning option, and discussing its implications with their clients. Be prepared to participate.

Chapter Six

—

RULE #6

COMMUNICATE! COMMUNICATE! COMMUNICATE!

You've all heard that only three things matter in real estate: "location, location, location." For estate planning, it's "communicate, communicate, communicate!"

First, you need to communicate *with other professionals.* Take each of your team members to lunch every six months. It will give you a great opportunity to share new ideas. I remember having lunch with an advisor, Jim, about a year ago. He brought me an article on "rolling GRATs," which I read with interest and continue to share with select clients, all the while crediting Jim. When you get together with others on your team, you'll also be taking advantage of what I call the "last lunch" rule: Chances are, the next time a team member has a referral, they'll think of you rather than the person they had lunch with two years ago.

Second, you need to communicate *with your clients.* Update them about important estate planning developments and changes in the law. Make it clear you're looking out for their best interests, and that you care about their personal situations.

Finally, you need to communicate *with potential clients*. I find that one of the most effective ways of doing this is to sponsor estate planning seminars, with an estate planning attorney, if possible. And always remember this: Everybody is a client. Some people just don't know it yet!

FINALE

There are 78 million "baby boomers" in our society approaching retirement age. As of 2008, people over the age of 50 have become the dominant economic power in the United States. According to Deloitte & Touche USA LLP, "Those that ignore this massive demographic shift and its global impact are likely to miss a significant opportunity."[1]

Now is the time to prepare yourself to meet the changing needs of this population. If you are unable to identify basic issues associated with estate planning or work effectively with your clients' estate planning attorneys and other financial service providers, your clients will quickly find other, better-informed advisors.

You can't learn what you need to know about estate planning in a day, but neither do you have to know everything to serve your clients well and become a valuable member of the estate planning team. It's possible that Chapter 3 in this book, "Tackle the Fundamentals," is completely new information to you. As with any unfamiliar subject, keep rereading this material until it starts to make sense.

The glossary on the next few pages will serve as a handy reference. Other resources such as seminars and profession-

---

1   Source: Deloitte & Touche USA LLP, Jan. 9, 2006

al articles will add to your knowledge, and eventually your growing experience will distinguish you as a superior financial advisor.

I love what I do. I help people. It's not always easy, but it is rewarding. I hope I've taught and inspired you about estate planning. Now it's up to you: Go make it happen!

Good luck.

Glossary

—

ESTATE PLANNING TERMS

"A" Trust: A subtrust established at the first spouse's death to hold assets in excess of the federal estate tax exclusion amount. The trust qualifies for the unlimited marital deduction, so no estate tax is due on the first death. When the surviving spouse dies, all assets in the "A" Trust pass to the children (or other named beneficiaries), but are included in the surviving spouse's gross estate for estate tax purposes.

A/B Trusts: The two subtrusts created upon the death of the first spouse that allow for use of the decedent's federal estate tax exclusion, and the unlimited marital deduction from estate tax.

Administrator: The person appointed by the probate court to serve as fiduciary of an estate of an individual who (i) died without a Will, or (ii) died with a Will but no executor was named or can serve.

Alternate Valuation Date: The date six months after a person's death that can be used for valuing assets on the estate tax return. It is used typically where the value of the assets is lower six months after the date of death.

Ancillary Administration: Probate proceedings in another state. Required when a decedent owns real estate outside his or her state of residence.

Annual Gift Tax Exclusion: The amount that an individual can transfer to another individual each year without gift tax consequences (currently $12,000, or $24,000 for married couples [see "split gift" below]).

Attorney-In-Fact: The person designated to act on behalf of an individual signing a Durable Power of Attorney.

Basis: The cost of property when purchased (or the fair market value of property when inherited), with certain adjustments for improvements and depreciation. If an asset is sold during the owner's lifetime for more than the basis, capital gains tax is due. If an asset is gifted during the owner's lifetime, the person receiving the gift takes the donor's basis in the property (referred to as "carryover" basis). With limited exceptions (most notably, certain retirement accounts), if an asset is left to a beneficiary at death, the basis for the beneficiary is stepped up to the fair market value of the property as of the date of death. In 2010, however, the amount stepped up at death is scheduled to be limited to $1,300,000 per decedent, with an additional $3,000,000 to a surviving spouse.

Beneficiary Determination Date: September 30 of the year following a retirement account owner's date of death. The date used for determining the beneficiary(ies) for "stretch" planning purposes.

Beneficiaries: The individuals or entities entitled to receive benefits from a Will, trust, insurance policy, annuity or retirement account.

Bequest: Something left at death in a Will or trust.

"B" Trust: A subtrust created at the first spouse's death to hold the federal estate tax exclusion amount. Upon the surviving spouse's death, all assets in the "B" Trust pass to the children (or other named beneficiaries) estate tax free.

Bypass Trust: Synonym for "B" Trust, Credit Shelter Trust and Family Trust (See "B" Trust above).

Capital Gain: Profit from the sale of an asset in excess of the basis.

Carryover Basis: (See Basis)

Charitable Gift Annuity: A contract in which an individual gives an asset to a charity, in exchange for the charity's making regular annuity payments to one or more beneficiaries for life.

Charitable Remainder Trust (CRT): A trust (established for a specific number of years or for a specified life or lifetimes) that provides lifetime income to the donor's designated beneficiaries, with the remaining principal passing to charity at the end of the trust term.

Charitable Lead Trust (CLT): A trust (established for a specific number of years or for a specified life or lifetimes) that provides income to a certain charity or charities, with the remaining principal passing to the donor's designated beneficiaries at the end of the trust term.

Codicil: A written amendment to a previously executed Will.

Credit Shelter Trust: Synonym for "B" Trust, Bypass Trust, and Family Trust (See "B" Trust above).

Crummey Letter: A written notification sent to each beneficiary of an irrevocable trust whenever a contribution is made to the trust. The letter gives the beneficiaries a period of time (usually 30 days) to withdraw a specified amount of the contribution. The withdrawal right gives the beneficiaries a present interest in the irrevocable trust, which is required for the contribution to qualify for the annual gift tax exclusion.

Decedent: A person who has died.

Deed: A document that transfers real property from one person or entity to another.

Disclaimer: A person's irrevocable written refusal to accept something left to him or her by Will, trust, or beneficiary designation. In order to be a "qualified" disclaimer under federal law, certain formalities in drafting, executing, and delivering the disclaimer must be met; the recipient must not have exercised any control over the disclaimed asset; and, with limited exception, the disclaimer must be made within nine months of death.

Donee: The recipient of a gift.

Donor: An individual or entity that makes a gift.

Durable Power of Attorney: A document whereby an individual designates another person to act on his or her behalf with respect to financial matters. The document terminates automatically upon the individual's death.

Durable Power of Attorney For Health Care: A document whereby an individual designates another person to act on his or her behalf with respect to routine health care decisions, typically in the event that the individual is incompetent to do so.

Dynasty Trust: An irrevocable trust drafted to exist in perpetuity, thereby avoiding estate and generation-skipping tax for future generations.

Estate: For estate tax purposes, the whole of one's property and possessions at the time of death. It also is used to refer to those assets that are subject to the probate process. For example, life insurance proceeds payable to a named beneficiary are not part of an individual's probate estate, but are includable in the individual's taxable estate for estate tax purposes.

Estate Tax: A tax imposed by the federal government upon the fair market value of the estate of a deceased person. The tax must be paid within nine months of death. Many states also impose their own estate tax.

Executor: The person named in a Will to handle the probate of a decedent's estate.

Fair Market Value: The price that a willing buyer would pay a willing seller, neither being compelled to buy or sell, and both being fully informed of all relevant facts.

Family Trust: Synonym for "B" Trust, Bypass Trust, and Credit Shelter Trust (See "B" Trust above).

Federal Estate Tax Exclusion: The amount that can pass to anyone at death free of federal estate tax. Under current law, the federal exclusion is $3,500,000 for 2009, dropping to $1,000,000 in 2011, with no estate tax in 2010.

"Ferrari" Trust: My colloquial term for a trust set up to prevent a beneficiary's unwise spending of his or her inheritance. See Testamentary Trust.

Fiduciary: A person or entity serving in a representative capacity. Executors, trustees, guardians, and agents under powers of attorney are all examples of fiduciaries. Anyone acting in a fiduciary capacity has a legal obligation to act in good faith, to follow the terms of the document appointing him or her, and to serve the interests of the beneficiary or beneficiaries diligently.

Generation-Skipping Tax (GST): A federal tax imposed, with limited exceptions, when a gift or bequest passes to someone more than one generation removed (e.g., a grandchild or more remote descendant, or a non-lineal descendant who is more than 37½ years younger than the person making the gift or bequest).

Gift Tax: A tax imposed on gifts made during one's lifetime. In addition to the annual gift tax exclusion amount (see above), each individual has a lifetime gift tax exclusion amount of $1,000,000, which is applied against the federal exclusion amount available at death. There is unlimited gifting between U.S. citizen spouses.

Grantor: Synonym for Settlor. A person who establishes a trust.

Grantor Retained Annuity Trust (GRAT): An irrevocable trust in which the grantor retains the right to receive a fixed annuity amount each year, usually for a term of years. At the end of the term, the remainder beneficiaries receive the remaining trust principal. Use of a GRAT allows for leveraged gifting because the amount of the gift is calculated based on the remainder interest.

Guardian: An individual with legal authority over another, typically a minor child.

Heir: Someone who inherits from the estate of a person who died without a valid Will.

Intangible Personal Property: Assets that can't be physically touched, such as stocks, bonds, bank accounts, mutual funds, and business interests.

Intentionally Defective Irrevocable Trust (IDIT): An irrevocable trust to which the grantor sells a discounted asset in exchange for a promissory note. Because the trust is a grantor trust, the grantor is treated as the trust owner for income tax purposes, and the sale between the grantor and the IDIT is "disregarded" for income tax purposes.

Inter Vivos Trust: A trust set up during a person's lifetime.

Intestate/Intestacy: Dying without a valid Will. As a result, the decedent's estate is distributed in accordance with state law.

IRD: Income in Respect of a Decedent: The income tax due on withdrawals from retirement accounts upon a person's death.

Irrevocable Life Insurance Trust: A trust established for the purpose of excluding insurance proceeds from the taxable estate of the insured.

Irrevocable Trust: A trust that may not be amended or revoked.

Joint Tenancy: A type of ownership whereby two or more persons own undivided interests in property, with the condition that upon the death of any joint tenant, the interest of the deceased joint tenant passes to the surviving joint tenant(s).

Life Estate: A right retained as part of a transfer of land. The owner retains the right to use and possess the land during his or her lifetime. Under federal estate tax law, the gross estate of a person holding a life estate must include the full value of the property subject to the life estate.

Living Trust: Synonym for Revocable Trust. A trust created during a person's lifetime, primarily to avoid probate. May be amended as long as the person is alive and competent.

Living Will: A document that sets forth an individual's wishes regarding the use of life-support and/or a feeding tube in the event he or she becomes terminally ill or permanently unconscious.

Marital Deduction: An unlimited deduction against estate tax and gift tax for the value of assets passing to a spouse.

Marital Trust: Synonym for "A" Trust and QTIP Trust (See "A" Trust above).

Net Unrealized Appreciation (NUA): The difference between the original cost basis and the fair market value of employer stock transferred out of a 401(k) account. If the employer stock is withdrawn from the 401(k) and transferred into a brokerage account (rather than rolled into an IRA), ordinary income tax is due only on the original cost basis. When the employer stock is subsequently sold, any appreciation is subject to capital gains tax, not ordinary income tax.

Probate: The court process whereby a decedent's assets are distributed to the appropriate beneficiaries. If a person dies with a Will (i.e., "testate") the assets are distributed in accordance with the terms of the Will. If a person dies without a Will (i.e., "intestate"), state law dictates who receives the assets.

Probate Estate: The assets that have to go through probate. Assets held in joint tenancy with rights of survivorship avoid probate. In addition, retirement accounts, proceeds of life insurance policies, and annuities are not part of the probate estate unless the beneficiary designation specifically lists the decedent's estate (never do that!).

Pour-Over Will: A Will used in conjunction with a Revocable Trust. Serves as a "safety net" to catch any assets (other than beneficiary designated assets) not retitled in the name of the Revocable Trust prior to the decedent's death. The beneficiary named in a pour-over Will is the decedent's Revocable Trust. Assets caught by the Will are "poured over" into the Revocable Trust after going through probate, and are then distributed to the beneficiaries named in the Revocable Trust.

Power of Appointment: A legal power given to a trust beneficiary. It authorizes the beneficiary to leave his or her beneficial interest in the trust to someone else, including a charity (the "appointee"), in the event he or she dies prior to the trust's ending. A "general" power of appointment places no restrictions on whom the beneficiary can name as appointee. As a result, assets subject to a general power of appointment are includable in the beneficiary's gross estate for estate tax purposes. A "limited" power of appointment places certain restrictions on whom the beneficiary can name as appointee. As a result, assets subject to a limited power of appointment are not includable in the beneficiary's gross estate for estate tax purposes.

Qualified Terminable Interest Property (QTIP) Trust: Synonym for "A" Trust and Marital Trust (See "A" Trust above)

Qualified Domestic Trust (QDOT): A marital trust used for a non-citizen spouse. Differs from a QTIP Trust in that withdrawals from a QDOT during the surviving non-citizen spouse's lifetime are immediately subject to federal estate tax.

Qualified Personal Residence Trust (QPRT): An irrevocable trust into which a client transfers his or her primary residence or second home. The client retains the right to use the property for a term of years, and then, at the end of that term, the real estate passes to his or her children (or other beneficiaries) at a discounted value.

Qualified Subchapter S Stock Trust (QSST): A trust qualified under federal law to hold subchapter S stock.

Real Property: Land and anything permanently attached to it.

Remainder Interest: An interest that comes into effect only after something else occurs. For example, suppose a client sets up a trust for his wife's benefit during her lifetime. When his wife dies, whatever remains in the trust passes to the children. The children have a remainder interest in the trust.

Required Beginning Date (RBD): The date on which an individual must begin taking minimum distributions from certain retirement accounts. With limited exceptions, the required beginning date is April 1st of the year following the calendar year in which the account owner turns 70½.

Revocable Trust: A synonym for Living Trust. A trust created during a person's lifetime, primarily to avoid probate. May be amended as long as the person is alive and competent.

Settlor: Synonym for Grantor. A person who creates a trust.

Split Gift: A gift made by a married couple, where more than the annual gift tax exclusion amount (currently $13,000) comes from one spouse's assets. A gift tax return is required, even if the amount gifted does not exceed $26,000. Restrictions apply for non-citizen spouses.

Tangible Personal Property: Items a person can touch, such as cars, furniture, jewelry, clothes, artwork, collectibles, boats, planes, etc.

Tenancy in Common: A means by which two or more persons own fractional interests in real or personal property. Upon the death of a tenant in common, his or her fractional interest passes to the beneficiaries named in his or her Will or Revocable Trust, or to his or her heirs if he or she dies without a Will or Revocable Trust.

Testamentary Trust: A trust created in a Will or Revocable Trust that does not come into effect until the death of the testator or grantor.

Testate: Dying with a valid Will.

Testator(m)/Testatrix(f): A person who makes a Will.

Title: Evidence of land ownership, documented by a deed recorded at the County Registry of Deeds.

Trust: A legal agreement by which assets are held by one person or entity for the benefit of another.

Trustee: The individual or entity holding title (in a fiduciary capacity) to assets in a trust.

Will: A document governing the distribution of a decedent's probate estate.

About the Author

—

SALLY MULHERN, J.D.

Sally received her law degree in 1982 from Cornell Law School, and her undergraduate degree, *summa cum laude*, Phi Beta Kappa, from Boston College in 1979. She is a founding partner in the law firm of Mulhern & Scott PLLC, with an office in Portsmouth, New Hampshire. Sally concentrates in sophisticated estate planning techniques, is a Fellow of the American College of Trust and Estate Counsel, and has been selected by her peers as one of Woodward & White's *The Best Lawyers in America*. She is also a member of Outstanding Lawyers of America. She speaks nationally to global financial institutions, universities (1999 and 2006 Cornell University keynote speaker on estate planning), charities, trust departments, financial advisors and professional organizations. Sally has spoken three times at Million Dollar Round Table (MDRT), and was a main platform speaker at the AALU Annual Meeting in Washington, DC, where she shared the podium with Colin Powell and James Carville. She is regularly quoted in the regional and national press, and recently appeared on *CBS MarketWatch* and in *The Wall Street Journal*.

Sally lives in Portsmouth, New Hampshire, with her husband, David (also a founding partner of Mulhern & Scott, PLLC). Sally and David have two adult sons.

Hire Sally as a Speaker for Your Next Conference!

Let her incredible **99+% audience approval rating** generate the results you're looking for!

Look at what people are saying about Sally's presentations:

"If it's results you're looking for, Sally's action-packed, effervescent presentation style coupled with her wisdom, knowledge, and deep understanding of complex issues makes her a 'must have' presenter for any occasion."

Jim McCarty
Vice President, American Express Financial Advisors

"You should know that I have heard nothing short of rave reviews about your enjoyable and informative presentation. I appreciate your willingness to share your expertise…, and for doing so with such extraordinary grace and humor."

Hunter R. Rawlings III
President, Cornell University

"Dynamic speaker! One of the best presenters we have ever had. Worth every penny!"

Vincent T. Cloud,
Executive Vice President/Chief Marketing Officer, Mutual Service Corporation

Here are some typical comments from participants:

"I thought Sally's presentation (as well as the materials she supplied) was one of the absolute best presentations I have ever attended, on any subject for that matter, in my 14 years in the insurance and investment business."

"Electrifying! The best speaker I've heard in years!"

"Really excellent. Leading edge. Way to go!"

"Had all of the key elements: participation, enthusiasm, knowledge, ability to field questions effectively, and humor."

continued

Sally is happy to customize a presentation to meet your particular needs. Here is a list of sample programs:

Estate Planning To Die For®:
Top 10 Ways to Increase Your Revenues

Estate Planning To Die For®:
Doing a Booming Business with Baby Boomers

Estate Planning To Die For®:
Turning Tax Law Uncertainty into Increased Sales

Charitable Estate Planning: Doing Well by Doing Good

Estate Planning To Die For®: Distribution of Retirement Benefits

How To Disinherit Uncle Sam:
Sophisticated Federal Estate Tax Planning

All In The Family:
From Private Foundations To Perpetual Dynasty Trusts

The 10 Key Elements of Estate Planning Success

e-Estate Planning: Issues and Solutions For The New Economy

Estate Planning Workshop: Join the Team

An Introduction to Estate Planning With Trusts

For information about Sally's fees and availability, please contact her:

Sally Mulhern
155 Fleet St.
Portsmouth, NH 03801

603-436-1211 • 603-436-1242 (FAX)
sally@mulhernlaw.com